Selling with

EASE

**The Four Step Sales Cycle Found in
Every Successful Business Transaction**

Chris Murray

Lucrum House Publishing

First published 2016

© Chris Murray 2009, 2010, 2011, 2012, 2013, 2014, 2015

Lucrum House also publishes books in a variety of electronic formats. Some content that appears in print may not be available in electronic books.

Publisher's note
Every possible effort has been made to ensure that the information contained in this book is accurate at the time of going to press, and the publishers and author cannot accept any responsibility for any errors or omissions, however caused. No responsibility for loss or damage occasioned to any person acting, or refraining from action, as a result of the material in this publication can be accepted by the editor, the publisher or the author.

ISBN-13: 978-1-849-14693-7
ISBN-10:   1-849-14693-4

Edited by; Daniela Nava
Cover Design by: Kumar V Vasu Sha
Interior Design by: Completely Novel

This book is for you, the salesperson reading this, endlessly knocking on doors, making phone calls and shaking stranger's hands – and wondering why so few people are willing to share those precious few principles, skills and techniques that would enable you to walk away with every possible opportunity from each and every sales call – and allow you to achieve your true potential.

And with all my love and thanks to Brian and Edith

And most of all, this book is for SJ, EJ and AC

Contents

FOREWORD

by **JEB BLOUNT**

Bestselling Author of

Fanatical Prospecting **and** *People Buy You*

It's been said that any fool can make the simple complex. Sadly, most authors who write about sales these days (with a few notable exceptions) feel compelled to complicate the simple and falsely promise that their formula will make sales easy. Given the proliferation of much of this worthless, confusing, and contrived advice, it's no wonder that so many salespeople are confused and failing at the craft.

Sales is simple. Not easy mind you. Simple. It's a process. A science that works like a well-oiled machine. Yes there is art but the art is embedded in the emotional intelligence required to effectively connect with other people, build relationships, and influence behavior.

In *Selling with EASE* Chris Murray, for lack of a better phrase, "keeps it real." He gives you core, tried and true, sales frameworks and shows you exactly how to apply them in the sales process. Along the way you get coaching on the art of selling; techniques that help you connect with your prospects, gain a deep understanding of their situation, and build solutions that are unique to them.

I love Murray's frameworks for:

- Opening sales conversations
- Asking strategic and artful questions that get below the surface and uncover real problems
- Connecting problems with solutions so that prospects perceive you to be an expert
- Adeptly closing the deal by pulling your prospect towards you on their terms
- Effectively dealing with objections and questions that may be holding you back

Selling with EASE is a handbook that will help you close more deals, advance your career, and build your income. I call it a handbook because unlike many books that gather dust on your shelves, you'll carry *Selling with EASE* in your bag and reference it often. Most importantly, this phenomenal book will become more valuable to you over time as you read the chapters again and again and highlight the pages.

- Jeb Blount
January 2016

"Inside the cold call is an appointment;
inside the appointment is an objection;
inside the objection is a need;
inside the need is a beautiful sale."

1 | INTRODUCING "SELLING WITH EASE"

EASE Selling – Just Another Gimmick?

"Selling with EASE" – sounds too good to be true, doesn't it?

In fact, isn't that kind of title the first cheap trick used by all those unscrupulous authors who hoodwink the unsuspecting public into making a purchase?

Well, dear reader, not me. I genuinely didn't call this book *Selling with EASE* simply to lure you into the first couple of pages and make a quick sale.

You see, I have no wish to be categorised as one of the many charlatans out there, all trying to sell self-help snake oil to decent people like you: that small group who have enough get-up-and-go to try to expand their understanding of a much derided subject, and to continue to look for some way to improve themselves and their fortune.

To be fair, if I'd written a book called *Selling Is Quite Difficult*, fewer people would have probably bought it, so you have got me there – but that's really not the reason for the title.

One of the major motivations for starting my training company, Varda Kreuz, and then for writing this book was to demystify, strip down and, wherever possible, simplify the sales process.

EASE is just an acronym. An acronym that I created when we first started coaching sales teams. And since we started to put it to use, those four letters have helped thousands of people – just like you – to understand that the sales process is actually built on four easily explained foundation stones, together with a small number of core pillars and principles, which extend out from those foundations.

I am well aware that selling is regularly (and quite rightly) presented in many formats as both a science and an art. In certain other works it is laid out as an everyday occurrence that everyone partakes in at some time; for example, parents sell the idea of going to bed at a decent hour to their children, while the kids try to sell the idea of staying up a little longer to their parents.

And it's true to say that, in many instances, the words "sell" and "influence" are completely interchangeable. Everybody sells something to somebody every day, whether it's a product, a service or just a case of making sure that they get their own way.

My sales career has been a mix of great advice (wasted on me in my youth), a number of personal discoveries (eureka moments that really should have come about a lot sooner), and (far more regularly) falling flat on my face, picking myself up and then learning from the experience.

Fairly early on in my career I realised that I had to learn more and improve myself in order to change my trajectory and become as successful as my aspirations showed me I could be. But when I first began to work my way through the shelves of the local library and bookshop, I quickly discovered that the information available fell into two quite distinct camps.

Some of the books that were recommended to me had a joy-eroding academic heaviness to the content. Although having them on my bookshelf made me feel fabulously intellectual, they felt instantly dreary and unreadable to the younger, attention span-deficient me – a young man who essentially wanted instant results so that he could go out and have some fun.

At the other end of the spectrum I discovered a selection of pop-culture books that dressed the sales process up to be some kind of mystical secret or ground-breaking new system. What all the works in this second camp usually had in common was a tendency to market themselves as the possessors of some preposterous one-line Jedi Mind Trick, which invariably never really worked in real-life sales situations.

Actually, before we go on – just so we're clear – nowhere in this book will you find a magic sentence that will close every sale. Do you know why?

Because they don't exist!

Think about it: if someone had found a way to manipulate human choice and free will – if someone actually had *that* kind of power – wouldn't it be a tad surprising if they then decided to share their secret with the masses for $20? Not to mention how it would be just very slightly unethical.

Admittedly, I understand that mind control might sound fairly attractive if you simply want to take money off your fellow man without ever understanding anything about them or helping in any way whatsoever (actually, I think that definitely must be unethical, illegal – or both – in most cultures). But surely you must also realise that, if *you're* going to be allowed to use this mind-controlling monologue on all of your prospects then other people will also be able to use it on you.

We're all somebody's prospect; we're all somebody's customer. Do you think you'd be the only person who'd use it to sell things?

This just goes to show why that concept is complete nonsense and terribly flawed. We'd all get rich by selling things that nobody actually wanted, but end up giving our fortunes away again to similar brainwashing con artists who filled our homes with equally useless tat.

So, I'll put my flag in the sand: **I believe that great selling involves helping people to make great buying decisions.**

It's about being able to work out what they really want and need, together with the skills and confidence to show them why they should purchase the product, service or solution that your business provides, rather than choosing the competition.

They get exactly what they need, while you hit your sales targets and become incredibly successful – fair deal.

Therefore, if you want to understand how to achieve sales and business success as effectively and professionally as possible, please read on. However, if you're after an easy way to hoodwink your prospect list into handing over their hard-earned money for a bag of magic beans, put this slender tome back on the bookshelf, my friend, as it's probably not for you. No snake oil to be found here.

In fact, if it doesn't work in real life, you won't find it in this book.

One final point before we crack on: while you read this, it may occur to you that certain parts appear a little obvious or simply common sense – and to be fair, you wouldn't be the first person to mention it.

But if that's true, then it surely exposes a slight paradox.

While writing this book, I endeavoured to lay out a blueprint and framework that will help those who read it to become commercially successful salespeople. However, in order to achieve that, I've also tried to explain what it feels like to be on the other side of the table – as a customer – thus explaining how we would all like to be treated by salespeople when we are customers ourselves.

If some of the content here feels like common sense then maybe it is to some. But I can't help wondering why customers (and that includes you and me) find it so difficult to recall more than a couple of occasions when they felt that they were treated exceptionally by the salespeople who dealt with them.

So, either the majority of the sales world knows exactly what to do and chooses to ignore it completely (losing business and future opportunities) or that *sense* isn't as common as some people think it is. If the latter is the case then the information required might benefit from being broken down, simplified and re-explained – and then implemented effectively by those at the frontline.

The Four-step Process

So what are these four fabulous foundation stones that make up the acronym **EASE**?

They are:
- **E**arn the right
- **A**sk the appropriate questions
- **S**olve the problem
- **E**xecute the solution.

As shown in the diagram, the four foundations are surrounded by an outer circle, which is split between **Commitment** at the top and **Understanding** at the bottom.

Let me explain a little further…

Earn the Right
A Commitment to Be the Sales Professional that Your Customer Really Needs

Quadrant one focuses on recognising why customers can fall over themselves to do business with certain salespeople, and yet take an instant dislike to so many others.

As you'll see from the diagram, the upper section of the cycle is bordered by the word COMMITMENT. It is during quadrant one that the salesperson proves they are the best choice to help the customer to achieve their vision.

This is all about committing ourselves to helping the customer.

Although dismissed by many, this step is vitally important: if customers don't trust you to help them at the beginning of the process, they certainly won't trust you with their money at the end of it.

Ask the Appropriate Questions
Understanding Exactly What Your Customer Is Trying to Achieve

As we move into the bottom half of the Selling with EASE cycle, the focus switches from commitment to understanding.

It's in quadrant two that you're going to develop a thorough understanding of what the customer is trying to achieve: what they want and need – and why.

Understanding a situation well enough to present a solution requires a particular set of questioning skills and techniques, as well as the much less talked about – but equally important – ability of effectively listening to the answers.

Solve the Problem
Helping the Customer to Understand Why You're the Best Person for the Job

Quadrant three continues round through the UNDERSTANDING half of the cycle. It's at this point that the focus turns away from working out the requirements of the customer and moves on towards helping them to understand how you propose to help.

Once you've diagnosed the problem, you need to know what you have within your portfolio that will deliver the customer's desired outcome. This is when you will need a whole new toolbox of skills to ensure that your message is presented as professionally – and received as effectively – as possible.

This isn't just about learning how to stand in front of a 50-slide presentation designed six months ago by your marketing team. Although, of course, getting the information across is important, you also need to be able to communicate with different personality types, recognise their buying motives and overcome their objections.

Execute the Solution
Gaining Customer Commitment and Delivering on Your Promises

As we move into the final quadrant of the sales cycle, we find ourselves back in the top half of the diagram, underneath the word COMMITMENT.

Once the customer understands how you can "Solve the problem", you will need to agree on a course of action that effectively results in their commitment to move forward, so that you can "Execute the solution". Amongst other things, this will involve: asking for the business, negotiating the best possible terms, filling in the required paperwork and staying true to your word.

© 2012 Ted Goff

"Every step of the sales process went perfectly except the part where the customer buys our product."

2 | EARN THE RIGHT

A Commitment to Be the Sales Professional that Your Customer Really Needs

Quadrant one focuses on recognising why customers can fall over themselves to do business with certain salespeople, and yet take an instant dislike to so many others.

As you'll see from the diagram, the upper section of the cycle is bordered by the word COMMITMENT. It is during quadrant one that the salesperson proves they are the best choice to help the customer to achieve their vision.

This is all about committing ourselves to helping the customer.

Although dismissed by many, this step is vitally important: if customers don't trust you to help them at the beginning of the process, they certainly won't trust you with their money at the end of it.

The Chapter that Unsuccessful People Never Read

May I make a polite request?

Please don't skip past this part of the book just because it doesn't look as sexy as some of the later chapters.

I know that you really want to get to grips with some of the questioning techniques and tips on effective negotiating straight away, but there is something vitally important that I have to share with you right now, before we go a single page further.

This section will have an incredible effect on the success of every single sales call that you will make from this day on.

I mean it: these few pages are worth the price of the book alone. "Earn the right" is where a large percentage of the business that you currently find difficult to close is hiding. If you read, absorb and implement the advice in this section, you will vastly improve your hit rate – and on top of that, you will be vibrating at a frequency that 90% of other sales professionals can't even operate at.

Honestly, in my experience only one in ten salespeople ever gets this bit right – and yes, they're the most successful 10% in every industry.

And to make it even more appealing, if you ensure that you put this chunk of Sales Tetris in place first, all the other pieces just take their own positions naturally. However, if you implement only a fraction of it, your hit rate will diminish massively. Ignore it completely, as most people do, and every subsequent clever sales line or questioning technique will have no effect whatsoever.

So, come on, turn the page – I've got something amazing to share with you.

Let's Start With Closing

During the first morning of our training workshops, we take a little time to find out what those attending would most like to achieve, and a large percentage of them regularly remark:

"I just want to improve my closing – that's all I need really. If I could close more sales, everything else would fall into place."

This is partly true; however, the ability to close sales effectively has never been confined to the last few moments of the conversation. It certainly doesn't magically take place in the fourth quarter of the sales process just because that's where the salesperson has it written down on their agenda, nor does it happen by trapping someone with a clever question or by using a particular phrase.

The fabulous motivational speaker and author Anthony Robbins tells a great story about a meeting with one of his clients, a plastic surgeon. He arrives early and, while he's in the waiting room, picks up a book that the surgeon has written.

As Anthony Robbins turns the pages, he sees pictures of the most beautiful people on Earth, all surrounded by mathematical equations. This surgeon had actually worked out what it took to possess, and therefore also how to create, the perfect face.

It turns out that if the philtrum (the groove between your nose and top lip) is exactly the same size as your eye, your face is in perfect balance – the perfect face.

One millimetre out and you have an average face; two millimetres out (according to Anthony Robbins) and you're butt-ugly. One millimetre out! Isn't it amazing how something so small can make so much difference?

Let's change the analogy.

Imagine that you're sailing from Liverpool, in the UK, to New York and your course starts out just one degree off.

This won't eventually get you a little way outside New York or even in the same state – one degree off sees your tiny boat floating all the way up somewhere in Canada.

And it's the same with every sales situation you'll ever walk into.

Take a look at this diagram.

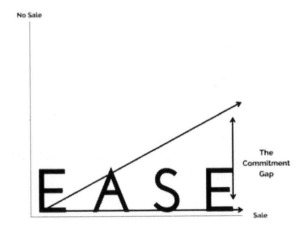

The line across the bottom represents the perfect sale.

You walk in, ask some great questions, show them the solution and they sign on the dotted line – well done you.

The line above that – the one going off at a jaunty angle – is where most sales appointments normally end up heading. That's the "one degree out" sales line.

It creates what I like to call the "commitment gap".

The commitment gap is the massive distance between "yes" and "maybe", and it's what generates the feeling of distrust that you have in the pit of your stomach when somebody is selling **AT** you rather than trying to help you make a great buying decision. It also represents what happens in all those appointments that seemed to be going brilliantly, but when you asked for the business, the prospect ended up saying something like:

> *"Do you know what? It sounds great, but I'm going to have to think about it."*

Planting the seeds for a commitment gap at the outset means that you will fail to gain the prospect's unspoken permission – to earn the right – to progress through the next three stages of the sales process.

Misjudge this quadrant by the tiniest degree and by the time you get to your well-practised close, you'll find yourself miles away from a "Yes", without even realising that anything had gone wrong.

Simply put: if you don't earn their trust at the beginning, they sure as hell won't trust you with their money at the end.

So, Do We still Need Salespeople?

Well, do we? Do we really still need salespeople?

Nowadays, you don't have to search very far to find an article, video or book declaring that selling is no longer relevant to modern-day business. Cold-calling is pronounced dead virtually on a daily basis, web-driven customer attraction techniques (without any salespeople involved) are almost guaranteed to be outdated before you finish reading this book and thousands of salespeople have recently faced the threat (or reality) of compulsory redundancy.

Truthfully, selling has acquired quite a bad name over the last few years – to be more precise, lazy practitioners and charlatans have given the art and science of selling a reputation that it really didn't deserve.

Ever since the internet made everything so easy and accessible way back in the mid-1990s, customers have started to cocoon themselves into their own private space. In this wonderful modern age, if you know what you want, you can just reach out and, with the click of a mouse, take complete control of your entire buying and shopping experience.

We no longer need to communicate or meet with other human beings who aren't in our personal circle of associates – we never need to climb out of our cocoon.

We've all got the internet.

That's why everybody looks so shocked if the telephone rings after a certain point in the evening – and God forbid that there should be a knock on the door after dark!

I don't know how far back you can remember, but that's not how it used to be when I was growing up. Back then, someone came along and knocked on our door almost every day: the insurance man, milkman, soda delivery guy, postman, scrap metal collector and window cleaner would all show up regularly – as did a rather scary, unwashed chap, with a contraption on the front of his bicycle, who offered to sharpen everyone's knives.

But that was then and this is now.

While I was writing this very page, a report pinged into my inbox; it forecasts that 22% of current business-to-business salespeople will be replaced by search engines within the next five years.

That got me to thinking: it's a myth that we don't need brilliant sales professionals. In fact, we desperately need them – far more than ever before – to help us, guide us, keep us informed and stop us from making diabolically stupid buying decisions.

The spectrum of choice available to us is vast and we generally don't realise how much our decisions are actually being quietly manipulated by the very technology that we think we're in control of.

Many people are already aware that if something is free on the internet then those using it – i.e. YOU and I – are somehow generating the revenue for its owner. But, of course, that's not how the majority perceive it. They like to believe that they're being guided unbiasedly by the caring and benevolent internet pixies.

So our cocoon gets increasingly snug and we stop telling strange salespeople about our problems; as human interaction starts to feel ever more uncomfortable and unnecessary, we slowly become progressively more guarded and untrusting of actual people.

After all, we all know that humans just want to rip us off and salespeople only look after themselves, right?

We can only trust ourselves and the impartial choices that the internet freely offers us.

So whether you've been in sales a while or you're just starting out, you need to recognise that things have changed dramatically. We need to "Earn the right" to become suppliers more than we ever did before.

Most pre-1990s hard-sell sales training no longer works on a twenty-first-century customer; if you sound like a contestant from *The Apprentice* or the customer believes that they are being sold AT, you have already failed.

You can no longer step into a sales job expecting an easy ride. Driving around and talking to people for a living, with no recognisable return for the time or money spent by your employer, is a job description that belongs in the past.

So ignore the people who say that the sales industry needs to become professionalised: it already has.

If you don't have the right attitude from day one, you are no longer welcome at the club. And in the twenty-first century if you don't hit the mark and tick all the boxes when you are given the chance, you won't last much longer than your induction month.

Truthfully, we all benefit from GREAT SALESPEOPLE but there isn't anyone anymore – customer or employer – who has any use for the other kind.

Salespeople Who Are no Longer Required

- Anyone who hasn't got the common decency to wash properly or can't be bothered to dress like a professional.
- Everyone who thinks that just turning up, pointing at a brochure and filling out an order form in return for a big salary, health care, expenses and a car is the formula for a long-term career.
- Those people who think that they're already the finished article – imbued at birth with some kind of sales superpower – and so never see sales as both an art and a science to be studied, polished and improved.
- Anyone who thinks that winning or getting one over on their fellow human beings is in some way clever.
- People who sneer at colleagues who try to improve themselves.
- All those who haven't invested any of their own time into understanding how their solution truly helps – and then complain that every buying decision is won or lost on price.
- Anyone who fails to recognise that if they go to see customers unprepared, without a plan, not completely believing in what they're selling or unable to explain why they're better than the competition then they are dreadful value for money for their employers (and a waste of time for prospects).

Salespeople that Every Employer and Prospect Desperately Want to Meet

- All those with humility, honesty, integrity, empathy and an old-fashioned work ethic that ensures the job gets done.
- Someone who understands the problem and can deliver a solution that works brilliantly for both sides.
- Anyone who has the tenacity to help people make great buying decisions and does it with the same enthusiasm shown by a small child who is describing the best Christmas present EVER.
- People who want to improve themselves in their own time and at their own expense, and whose personal goal is to be the best.
- All those who deliver value that wasn't there before they arrived.

The Jedi Mind Trick for Salespeople

I once had a colleague who referred to the expectations of some salespeople and their managers as requiring *"magic sales fairy dust"*.

This description has always made me smile.

Sadly, as I mentioned earlier, there are a number of authors and organisations out there who will happily sell the promise of "magic sales fairy dust" – and more than enough people lining up at their door to keep them in business.

Those expectations exist – and some people are willing to exchange their money for dust (no magic or fairies involved) – because we live in the fabulous age of the *"quick fix"*.

It's a hope thing.

Teenagers choose a cream that clears their skin of blemishes because they don't want to put any time or effort into using the preventative soap. When they get a little older, they want small electrical discs that promise them a washboard stomach without any need to exercise and, shortly after that, a pill to get thin rather than having to adopt a healthy lifestyle or diet.

In the same way, all those who haven't got time to learn how to communicate effectively want to believe that there is some business version of the Jedi Mind Trick. They are all looking for some easy-to-learn magical words and hand movements that will turn them into instant millionaires and world-class closers.

I can't and won't promise you magic sales fairy dust or the Jedi Mind Trick for salespeople – they simply don't exist.

However, before we even get into our stride, let me offer you five pieces of advice that – if you're willing to put in a little effort and implement them – will give your competition the impression that you possess a bag or two of something special.

Know HOW the thing that you sell helps *"THEM"*.
"Them" is your target market. What would make it worth for *"them"* to see you? It's probably not what you think.

Remember: when you walk into a DIY store to buy a drill, you don't want the drill. Your end goal is to make a hole and, in order to achieve this, you have to buy the drill.

Bad salespeople will take great delight in showing you all the drills they have to offer, but really great salespeople will spend their time asking you about the wall you're drilling into and what you need the hole for, and then match your need to an appropriate option.

In the same way, your target market probably don't care that much about the solution you're offering – they're more likely to be bothered about whether it will get them promoted, sacked, recognised, accepted, praised or laid.

Believe and trust in those benefits.
Don't tell me you're passionate about your job – show me that you're passionate about helping people like me.

Get up in the morning on a mission to save prospective clients from the shabby, ill-fitting, overpriced and worthless alternatives that your competitors are trying to get away with flogging them.

Only invest time in prospects you can REALLY help.
If what you sell doesn't help me then why are you knocking on my door?

You need to have "recognising *THEM*" down to a fine art.

Remember that if the real *them* don't end up as your customers, they're going to miss out somehow (see point 2 above) and you can't let that happen because that will weigh heavy on your conscience. So don't waste your time with people you can't help and concentrate instead on those you can.

You're going to become an expert at searching, filtering, focusing and making sure that the people who need to see you actually do get to see you.

Perception vs expectation.
A prospect won't move forward if they perceive that a solution delivers less than expected. It's at this point that you need to provide the required information which allows them to make a new decision.

This doesn't mean changing their mind; you'll never change anybody's mind.

You need to give them enough information to make a new decision, based on which their perception will change. If this new perception of a product, service or solution outweighs their initial expectation, they will be satisfied – otherwise, they won't.

Explain the value and justify the cost.
People don't mind paying; they just don't like to overpay.

As the great Zig Ziglar said:

> *"The genuine sales professional can't sell anything to anybody – that's a con artist."*

Salespeople who think that it's all about the price don't add anything to a sale: if a product is all about cost, it can be sold on the internet at the lowest price, with the huge costs of a sales team taken out of the equation.

Would You Buy from YOU?

An exercise at the beginning of my foundation level sales workshops asks the delegates to list which words they would use to describe the perfect salesperson.

The answers always tend to be a collection of emotive nouns and thrusty adjectives which conform to the stereotypical sales caricature, such as driven, persuasive, hard-nosed, tenacious, thick-skinned, results-orientated, relentless and "never takes no for an answer".

It is a rare moment indeed when anyone mentions the words honest, empathic, trustworthy, humble, reliable, helpful or customer-focused.

You might have got this far into the book and started to think that the whole idea of being customer-focused just isn't dynamic enough for you. I can imagine some of you thinking: *Come on, Chris, I started to read this to pick up a couple of tricks of the trade and sales techniques… to close a few more sales – don't start getting all sentimental and "meaning of life" on me.*

That's a fair point, but just for a moment stop thinking about the perfect salesperson you'd like to be in your *Wolf of Wall Street* daydream and instead try to focus on what you expect from those who are selling something *to* you.

The salesperson you'd ideally like to be and the salesperson you'd like to encounter as a customer should roughly be the same, shouldn't they? I reckon your perfect buying experience would rarely involve someone who has the skin of a rhino or is unnecessarily (even illegally) persuasive, would it?

Here are five reasons why a customer-focused approach has the ability to make your sales soar and – as an extra bonus – isn't half-bad for the soul either.

1. **You will increase customer loyalty.**
Customers want to spend their time with people they trust and believe in. They need someone they can count on. If that person is you, there's a fair chance that they'll stick around and buy something – and maybe come back again next time.

2. **You will start to build real relationships.**
Meaningful business partnerships, reciprocity, opportunities to increase your network and referrals: these are all good reasons for becoming recognised as "the one" when people need to speak to someone in your field of expertise.

3. **You reap what you sow.**
When you begin to focus on being honest with others – in business and life in general – you will start to find yourself surrounded by people who are also honest with you. Unfortunately, that doesn't mean roses round every door and streets lined with gold, but it does mean that you will focus on real opportunities and start moving yourself towards achieving goals that really matter to you.

4. **You can go back and sell to them again.**

Come on, be honest: are there some customers in that database that you'd rather not go back to because of the way you treated them last time?

5. **It's how you'd want to be treated.**

Often when you put on your sales hat – for some unknown reason – you completely forget how it feels to be a customer. Can you honestly say that you would like your next experience with a sales professional to be a carbon copy of how you just treated your last client?

Why not step out of your sales bubble for a few minutes and look at it from a different perspective. Make a list of the words that define how you expect to be treated when you're being sold to rather than how you think great salespeople should act.

It constantly amazes me how those two lists differ.

Maybe if we work to make the old sales cliché extinct – one salesperson at a time, and starting with ourselves – customers (and that includes you and me) will start being treated the way they deserve to be.

Would Your Customers Offer You a Job?

Here's an interesting way for you to set the bar professionally and work out whether your customers believe that you've earned the right to be viewed as a trusted supplier.

Just imagine that the unthinkable happens tomorrow: the company currently paying your wages collapses, gets sold or, completely out of the blue, decides to make 50% of the sales team redundant, including – (clearly) unjustifiably and unfairly – YOU!

QUESTION: would you be able to turn to your current customer base for a job?

Here is why this is an odd situation.
- Getting on really well with your customers might not actually help you.
- Having built a career doing them *"secret favours"* in the past almost certainly won't help you.
- Having consistently let them down in the past definitely won't help you.
- If you spent every waking moment ripping them off, absolutely nothing will help you.

The problem is that your present career trajectory might not be as definitive as you currently believe it to be. Although it's difficult to acknowledge this fact from where you're standing now, trust me: there are commercial cliff edges that for the time being remain hidden by the deceptive mist of recent wins and your own self-delusion.

Over time, successful salespeople develop a balance between looking after their customers (commercially and professionally) and consistently delivering the best possible deal back to the business that pays their wages.

So how do you become one of these uber-salespeople?

I'm glad you asked. The answer is really quite simple.

You look after your customers so well that, should the need arise and they can afford you …

They will hire you tomorrow!

In a heartbeat, without a second thought and no questions asked.

In order to achieve that, you've got to work out what customers respect in a salesperson.

Not what they like about you: what they **respect**.

Not whether they get the best price or deal: **respect**.

Then again, it's also worth remembering that they won't respect someone who always gives them a hard time. When you respect someone, you actually enjoy doing business with them.

Sometimes it's not possible to work together – so you don't – but that feeling of mutual respect should always be there.

Here is a list if of sales types that I can guarantee won't make an appearance on the shortlist.

Nobody respects a salesperson who:
- rolls over and gives an unnecessary or easy discount
- bad-mouths their current employer
- agrees with customers about their employer's faults
- constantly turns up late for appointments
- forgets to charge their laptop before seeing them
- isn't prepared for meetings
- sends proposals out late
- doesn't try to understand a customer's real needs
- doesn't keep their word
- sneers or looks down their nose at what they believe to be the second level of the supply chain
- doesn't understand the unwritten laws of business attire.

The customer should know that they have your respect from the beginning of your relationship. Equally, you need to go in there and earn their respect as soon as humanly possible.

One day we might all have to stand in front of one of our customers and ask for a job. So ask yourself: how confident would you be? If you had the choice, would you rather your customers respected your professionalism or simply liked you? And which alternative do you think would get you a job?

Here's my point: the actions that earn respect will also land the job and help to turn prospects into customers.

How to Give Your Customers a Good Night's Sleep

One of the most infuriating things – and saddest truths – about life in the twenty-first century is that nobody ever seems to want to help their fellow human beings.

You must have experienced it too sometimes...

- The guy who's in too much of a rush to let you out of that road junction during rush hour. (Would it kill them to leave a space?)
- The time you required a bit of customer service, but the customer service desk was clearly the wrong place to go looking for it.
- When you needed a work colleague from another department to drop in a good word for your promotion opportunity, but they were just too busy to remember.

This is a reality that buyers – customers and prospects – recognise more acutely than anyone else.

All the successful businesspeople you encountered last week desperately wanted someone to walk in and make their lives a little easier, take some weight off their already over-burdened shoulders and shine a welcome ray of light down a seemingly endless tunnel.

Do you know why? Nobody **EVER** does.

Those businesspeople might look brave and bold – it's part of their DNA, their personality types; that's the way they're wired – but, fairly regularly, you'll find that it can all just be a mask to hide a gritty reality.

If you could put on your business reality glasses, you'd see:
- the boss who is breaking her back, trying to keep the right balance between pleasing customers and staff
- the small business owner who spends every day trying to keep a roof over his family's head, while also continuing to help pay the mortgage of everyone he employs
- the CEO who wakes up at 3 a.m., worrying about problems that no one else in her organisation even knows about
- the head of the purchasing department who has nothing ground-breaking or new to present next quarter to a waiting boardroom.

Yet, without fail, every single day some schmuck walks in or rings up, with the sole aim of trying to take some money off them for a $50 box that isn't required and wasn't asked for – and even after the box is politely declined, they'll try a sure-fire, never-fail closing technique to win them over.

And the reason it just feels like bad selling is because that's exactly what it is.
- No one ever tries to solve a problem or scratch an itch – they just want to sell you stuff.
- No one ever comes in with the purpose of making your job easier – they just need to show you the new presentation.

- No one ever tries to help you make a great buying decision – they're just hoping that this box is what you're looking to buy today.

So if you want to stand out from the majority of salespeople, you simply need to start understanding why people buy your stuff and then work out how it helps them.

From the word go, you should try to help – selling should become a by-product of helping rather than the other way round.

Once you've made people aware that you're there to help, you've got to be ready to diagnose the problem accurately and present the solution in such a way that every bit of your explanation is completely clear. Finally, you should deliver the original promise and **help them**. No one else is doing that – no one else wants to do that – no one else cares enough to do that.

Let your competition continue carrying in that $50 box – you, my friend, are walking in holding the answer to your prospect's sleepless nights.

Why Trust and Confidence Matter so Much

Here are a couple of questions to start us off.

- If you felt unwell, would you follow the medical advice of a scruffy, inebriated man, sitting on a bed of old newspapers at the train station, who claimed to be a doctor?
- Would those of you with children go out for the evening and leave your kids with a complete stranger who knocked on the door the night before, asking if they could babysit?

Of course you wouldn't; you would require the trust and confidence that come with recognition, reputation and proof.

You know how salespeople and service providers make you feel when they engage with you. You instantly know whether you want to work with someone or not – and you're well aware of the ones you don't want anywhere near your business, home or family members.

It is vital to understand that any prospective customers (our fellow human beings) really want to find someone they can work with, someone they can trust.

Ideally, they would like someone to come along, answer their questions and take away their problems – but how do you think they feel when 80% of those who book appointments with them walk in looking like an unmade bed, forget to bring all the supporting information and tools required, and then do nothing but sell at them from the word go?

The Two Perceptions

Walking in through the large revolving front door of a prospect's office building can be a heart-pounding, uncomfortable moment for even the most seasoned salesperson. From the very first "hello" uttered at reception to the long walk as you're escorted to the meeting room, you can feel the effect of their scrutiny and possible disapproval gnawing at the pit of your stomach.

Even once you've said goodbye and found yourself back on the street, there are occasions when you feel that you've ended up with even less of a connection than before you'd met them.

However, you can easily avoid these difficulties if you know how to take ownership of the power used to create those feelings. In order to understand how to achieve that level of control, you need to be thoroughly aware of two perceptions before you embark on your next customer appointment, telephone conversation or even written correspondence.

Perception #1: How You Want to Be Perceived on Your Way in

It used to be said that you only have as long as it takes for a small match to burn down to your fingertips for you to make a first impression.

During those few seconds (never more than ten) people make countless judgements about you (it doesn't matter if they're right or wrong – that's how they see you) and after they have, it's a long, hard uphill battle to try to convince them that they're mistaken in any way.

Ask anyone who has had the misfortune of inviting an unshaven double-glazing salesman to take a seat in their lounge – shuffling in with his tatty unpolished shoes and a large sauce stain down the front of his unironed beige shirt – and they'll tell you straight away that they never trusted the quality of the windows being discussed.

In the twenty-first century, though, it's not just the way you look or present yourself that affects a first impression. You have to ensure that your online presence is stunningly professional too (they will definitely look you up before they meet you); you have to give the impression that you're organised and that your time is a precious and expensive commodity (which it is).

The big question you need to ask to ensure that you get this bit right is:

"What do I want them to think about me before I even open my mouth?"

Perception #2: How You Want to Be Perceived on Your Way out

Just for a moment, let's not think about what you have to achieve for your company, the amount you have to sell to hit your target or the creation of that 30-second killer introduction and gobsmacking presentation.

Instead, give yourself two minutes to decide how you want your customers and prospects to talk about you once you're no longer in the room. If all your customers got together for a big party to celebrate your career – and the incredible impact you've had on theirs – what would you want them to say about you in the speech before dinner?

Get a blank A4 piece of paper and jot down a rough copy of how you want to be perceived and remembered by this collection of all your customers – past, present and future. Write down the key phrases, feelings and observations that you'd like them to voice.

Now dig a bit deeper. If you've written words such as *professional*, draw lines that originate from those terms and explain what you actually mean by them. "Professional" means lots of different things to different people. How would anyone know that you are professional? What would you need to have done?

Lay out in front of you, on that piece of paper, the salesperson persona that you wish to be associated with in the minds of other people. Then the next time you're with a customer or prospect: **be that salesperson!**

The big question you need to ask to ensure you get this bit right is:

"How do I want them to talk about me, after I've left?"

A Couple of Ideas to Keep You on Track

- Look in the mirror – would you buy from you?
- Make sure that you've planned out where you intend to be over the course of the next month. Apart from the obvious time management advantages, you'll also appear to be busy and organised enough to be viewed by prospects as a competent and in-demand supplier.
- Understand the purpose of each and every call – don't waste your time or even think of wasting the time of your customers.
- The journal in which you write your notes, your pen, your presentation material and your laptop case – do they all scream *"I'm the person you should be doing business with"?*
- Charge everything that needs charging the night before. Also, always have enough business cards and all the marketing material that customers and prospects regularly ask for.
- Pick a winning, positive, helpful and friendly attitude – this alone will set you above 50% of other salespeople.
- When you visit prospects and customers, you're a guest – please act like one.
- Listen to, and interact with, the conversation that THEY want to have with you – don't talk about the drill that you've come in to sell; ask them about the hole that they're trying to create.

- Become the kind of salesperson that you'd personally recommend to your friends and family.

As Barnabas Kreuz points out in the book *The Extremely Successful Salesman's Club*:

"Let your customers and prospects recommend you to each other and let your competition wish they were you."

Concentrate on Great Execution

Every now and then, I find myself in a room with a group of salespeople who tell me that their life would be so much easier if:

- the quality of their product or service were somehow better
- their boffins created something a bit more cutting edge
- the competition offered them a job.

And more often than not, it's actually not their product or service that's at fault – it's the way they're selling it.

One of the eight secrets laid out by Felix Dennis in his book *How to Get Rich* is:

"Ignore great ideas. Concentrate on great execution."

It's a pretty massive statement for most salespeople to get their head round – where do you start?

In order to make it a little more understandable, I've put together an example using classic rock bands. In the diagram below there are four quadrants – with axes headed *"ideas"* and *"execution"* (on a scale of regular to great) – which have been populated with a selection of world-famous music acts.

Great Ideas

All the genius musicians you've ever met who never made it big	Rush Pink Floyd
	Jimmy Hendrix
	U2 Iron Maiden
	Led Zeppelin Rolling Stones
	Beatles The Doors
	The Who Queen
	Nirvana David Bowie

Regular Execution | Great Execution

All the guys at the pub with stories about a fleeting teenage rock career	Def Leppard AC/DC
	Ozzy Osbourne Kiss
	The Eagles Foo Fighters
	Aerosmith
	Guns n' Roses
	Motorhead Bon Jovi
	Sex Pistols Green Day

Regular Ideas

Before you start contemplating whether to throw this book to one side in disgust due to the fact that you believe the Beatles might have been more creative than Rush, let me explain: I created the diagram to prove the following point.

It doesn't necessarily matter what you're selling – it's the way you sell it that makes all the difference to your results.

Now don't get me wrong: selling tat that doesn't work is never a long-term career move – but neither is playing dreadful music.

Same result: no one buys it.

Nevertheless, isn't it amazing how so many people in so many disciplines and industries can still be extremely successful with something that just *"gets the job done"*?

You see, the main thing that all those bands have in common (drum roll, please) is: **great execution**.

They knew how to sell what they had to sell.

They looked great, they sounded great, they perfected their personas and external perception (whether those personas were true or not), they got themselves in front of the right people, and they continued to practise until their fingers bled.

So what does great execution look like in the context of a successful sales career? Well, it's definitely not a monologue of witty banter during a corporate golf day or or a solid hour of PowerPoint animation trickery.

It's about delivering value: for you, for your employers and for you customers.

- **Value for your customers**. Understand why people buy what you sell and then talk about – and deliver – that. Earn the right to be there, perfect the two perceptions (whether true or not), get yourself in front of people you can help and then help them.

- **Value for your employers**. You're either helping them grow and stay in business or you're in the way – keep bringing a bigger stick back (continuously, throughout your career) with your tail wagging and most will be more than happy to retain your services for the foreseeable future.

- **Value for you**. Make sure that you become the person you want to become and never stop working towards the goals in your life that you truly want to achieve. After all, don't you think that this precious, unrepeatable, glorious life – your life – deserves someone to execute it with all the greatness they can muster?

Things to Keep in Mind

This book isn't meant to be a self-help manual for sorting out your whole life, so we won't stray too far from the topic of selling; however, there are a number of key points that will really help you to concentrate on, and achieve, great execution.

Work out What's Most Important...

"Most important" is different from desperately urgent. What's important to you, your business and your customers might not be the thing that's constantly at the top of your to-do list. Work out the most important things that you, your business and your customers want to see happen this week, this month and this year, and then ensure that the busy winds of life don't end up blowing you off course.

... And then Measure Yourself Against the Numbers that Matter

Everybody plays the game differently when someone's keeping score. Find a way to measure what you're doing. Set yourself personal targets and then create a spreadsheet, log them on a whiteboard or just keep them in your diary. Remember: running slowly isn't giving up. The forward motion is what counts; moving forward, even in tiny steps, should always be classed as positive.

Why Your Next Sale Is More Important than Your Current One

You may be aware that when writing advertising copy, the real skill is to generate enough interest and cram enough quality into the first line that it's almost impossible not to want to read the second line. Then the second has to have exactly the same effect on the reader so that they continue on to third and then the fourth, fifth, and so on.

Well, here's my sales version and if you adopt this mindset, it will have a huge impact on your results. Instead of focusing on whatever it is that you're selling to your customer right now, try to concentrate on what you want to sell them next time, making sure that you achieve the sale *after* this one.

Take the pain and stress out of *this* sale and instead deliver the proposal that lays the foundation for a long-term relationship. It doesn't matter what you're selling – big, small, something worth millions of dollars or just a handful of change – the effect will always be the same.

If you went in thinking: *"I know you want to buy this one – that's a given – so that's not what I want to concentrate on. I'm just going to try to help you make the best choice possible and then deliver it to the best of my ability. I'm going to do such a good job for you with this sale that you will definitely buy the next one off me when you eventually decide that you need it,"* how do you think your style and content would be affected?

You get the next sale: by concentrating on customer satisfaction to that extent, matching their needs with benefits that really matter, delivering 100% of your promises and being there afterwards to make sure that there's nothing left that needs sorting out.

Interestingly, that's how you stand a better chance of getting this one too.

Nevertheless, I get it: for you young, thrusty wolves out there, who are all living in the NOW, it's all about the next big win.

Fair enough.

But when you start selling to ensure the future sale rather than the current one; when you decide that you want to help people to make great buying decisions rather than just selling at them; when you set your sights on (and recognise there's always) the long term – that's when the customers start to get something that they tell their friends about and you, my friend, will end up with an incredible career rather than a simple sales job.

The Sales Lessons that Every Ten-year-old Already Knows

You may have heard of a book called *All I Really Need to Know I Learned in Kindergarten*, by Robert Fulghum. It is a collection of short anecdotes, best known for the short piece relating to the title, where the author talks about the rules he learnt in his early years, which turned out to be equally relevant when he became an adult.

I had a similar epiphany while waiting to pick up my kids from school recently, as I read a large laminated set of rules hanging on the corridor wall.

In both my roles as Sales Director and Sales Coach, I have looked after individuals with a variety of skill sets over the last three decades, and I can honestly say that the things which set the 10% (those you would employ again and again) against the other 90% (who populate the rest of the industry) can all be found in the next 16 little nuggets of advice aimed originally at five- to ten-year-olds.

In my general behaviour I will try to:
- be polite, well-mannered and respectful
- act sensibly and safely
- use appropriate language
- be honest, even if I have done something wrong
- be trustworthy
- look after my belongings and avoid losing things
- keep my desk tidy

- take pride in my appearance.

When working, I will try to:
- arrive on time
- bring the correct books and equipment
- listen attentively
- get on with my work quickly, using my time effectively
- take an interest
- listen to what other people have to say and respect them
- take pride in the appearance of my work
- do my work to the best of my ability.

Ditch that Pitch for Something More Effective

Have you ever heard of an elevator pitch? Also referred to as a 30-second advert, this is a quick, scripted summary of your product or service and its value proposition.

The idea is that, should you be fortunate enough to find yourself bumping into an important prospect while riding the elevator, you'll be able to use those 30 seconds so effectively that they will want to continue the conversation with you long after reaching their floor.

This all sounds great on paper but, in reality, the copy-and-paste, monotone, emotionless and dead-behind-the-eyes delivery of most elevator pitches is, at best, horrifically insincere.

Until recently, I couldn't quite put my finger on why I disliked the average sales-trainer-taught elevator pitch so vehemently. I have no problem with the theory behind it; in fact, I completely understand the need for it, and many times in my youth I'd turn up at a networking event and wished I could succinctly get across how I'd helped my existing clients. I just knew in my heart of hearts that the way most of these pitches are executed could never deliver the results that they were intended to achieve.

Additionally, I always knew that if someone approached me at a networking event – or worse, cornered me in an elevator – and then proceeded to speak *at me* for half a minute, I would never willingly follow them, while they played their mystical sales flute. In reality, I would probably become uncharacteristically introvert and make my excuses just to get them out of my face.

Actually, my teeth are itching just thinking about it. But where were all the articles and quotes by the "Big names" on planet sales to back me up or use as a reference to argue my side logically?

Then lo and behold, the wonderful Seth Godin wrote a short piece on elevator speeches in his blog that summed up my feelings perfectly.

Here is my favourite bit:

"If you've told me what I need to know to be able to easily say no, I'll say no. The best elevator pitch doesn't pitch your project. It pitches the meeting about your project. It's not a practiced, polished turd of prose that pleases everyone on the board and your marketing team."

So whether you are getting in touch with people through social media, on the telephone, knocking on doors or attending organised networking events, start to create a conversation piece that gives them a real reason to have a proper discussion with you – comfortably, professionally – like genuine businesspeople do when they have something meaningful and important to talk about.

Think about it like this: if you're given the opportunity to speak with someone who will benefit from having a full consultative meeting regarding your product or service then... *You've got to learn how to pitch the meeting and NOT the meat.*

The *"Listen to me – listen to me! – buy now!"* content of most elevator speeches rarely contains enough space or direction to allow the prospect to move forward to the next stage of the journey.

Whether on the telephone or face to face, if the objective of this brief conversation is to book an appointment then make sure that in those precious seconds you convey the passion and belief of someone who is evangelical about their cause.

Most of the time, an elevator pitch is simply a chance to earn the right to move one step further forward in the sales cycle, so treat it as such and make sure that you take that step. It definitely isn't a 30-second commercial designed to stun the buying sense out of your fellow human being – because in the real world those don't work and never have.

The Truth about Relationship Selling

Relationship selling is a strange beast and countless authors have made many, many dollars explaining to salespeople how to use it to their advantage.

Here's a quick question for you:

Why would a professional buyer decide to meet with a new salesperson?

Is it because they don't have enough friends? Do you think they have seats that they just can't fill at their wedding or that they're trying to build a trade-only quiz team and they need someone with a sales background to be the captain?

Could it be that maybe – just maybe – they make their living by meeting people just like you and me, and are tasked with getting the best possible deal for the most suitable product or service?

It's just a thought.

This kind of thinking upsets an awful lot of people, but if you truly believe that business is mostly about relationships, let me ask you another question:

How many bad second-hand cars would you buy off your best friend?

A relationship can only take a business transaction to a certain point.

With that in mind, can we just take it as read that the sales department needs to be populated with people who are actually quite good with other people?

So let's move forward, without forgetting that in order to be an effective sales professional, it's crucial for you to be the kind of person who gets along with customers: polite, pleasant, empathetic and upbeat – someone everyone wants to spend time with. After all, we all have the choice to go elsewhere if it turns out that you're not. That's not about building relationships – it's just common business sense.

And that's *completely* different from saying that we should have the ability to worm our way into a customer's affection as if we were setting some Mata Hari honeytrap, pretending to like people just so we can get the desired results through manipulating those emotions.

In reality, you're never going to blackmail a professional buyer into something that isn't right for them by using friendship – and, if you think about it, that would be a fairly horrible thing to do anyway.

They have a job to do and if you want them to become a first-time or regular customer then you need to give them exceptional reasons for doing so. Strive to be viewed as valuable – rather than simply likeable – by engaging in activities and offering solutions that they see as being genuinely useful.

Becoming Evangelical

How do you feel when you first walk in to see, or pick up the telephone to call, a prospective customer?

What are you thinking and feeling while presenting your solution?

Zig Ziglar once said:

> *"Selling is essentially a transference of feeling."*

Simply put: if I can make you feel as excited and enthusiastic about my product or service as I feel then we'll have a supercharged conversation about solving your problem.

However, if you don't feel as excited and enthusiastic about my product or service as I do, we won't.

But there's a huge stumbling block with that idea and it's this; most salespeople don't feel anything about their product or service – nothing at all. Nobody has ever asked them to put a whole lot of thought into this aspect of the sales process. They're just sent out with a box to sell and they do their best to call on the people who are most likely to buy it.

So during their presentation, the message behind their eyes, the unspoken projection they're actually giving out, is something like: *"Do you like this? Go on, give me a clue. I need to sell you this. Would you like one?"*

Instead of: *"This is fabulous, amazing – I love it! You're going to like this just as much as me, I'm sure of it – I can't wait to show you. Frankly, I'm amazed you've lasted this long without one!"*

There are two things to take from the Zig Ziglar quote above. Firstly, most salespeople haven't realised how much they've helped their existing customers. So they feel like they're "bothering people" rather than helping.

Selling = annoying and getting in the way

instead of:

Selling = helping someone to make a great decision.

In our sales training workshops we talk about becoming evangelical.

Evangelists don't tell you about Heaven to get themselves there; they tell you because they're worried you'll miss out. As they're already going – that's not the worry – the sin would be for them *not* to share Paradise with other people. So they stand on street corners and in shopping malls with the Good Book in one hand and clutching their chest with the other, preaching with all their might.

They believe they have the perfect answer to all your questions – and so they do their very best to be heard. This is how you should be when talking about your product or service.

Once you've really worked out how you help people and why your product or service is better for them than any other, you'll realise that you'd be doing them a mighty disservice if you simply walked away without sharing the good news.

What you provide really helps someone, solves problems, eases a pain or delivers pleasure – the world needs what you've got, so why would you hold back?

In order to find the confidence you need, discover how you can help those people who buy from you – rather than learning how to sell at them – and then share your message with others, before the rest of the world gives them something inferior or just plain wrong.

Therefore, the second thing to take away from Zig Ziglar's quote is:

Make sure you have that feeling to transfer.

If you *feel* that you can help someone with what you sell, they'll feel it too. If you *feel* that yours is the best option for the customer then that is what will come across. The question is: what feelings and beliefs are you currently subconsciously sending out?

Are they helpful?

© 2000 Ted Goff

"No, I never heard the one about the salesman who wouldn't shut up and the busy purchasing executive with a short temper. How does it go?"

3 | ASK THE APPROPRIATE QUESTIONS

Understanding Exactly What Your Customer Is Trying to Achieve

As we move into the bottom half of the "Selling with EASE" cycle, the focus switches from commitment to understanding.

It's in quadrant two that you're going to develop a thorough understanding of what the customer is trying to achieve: what they want, need – and why.

Quadrant two is all about understanding the customer.

Comprehending a situation well enough to present a solution requires a particular set of questioning skills and techniques, as well as the much less talked about, but equally important, ability of effectively listening to the answers.

Avoiding an Anti-sales Structure

Right at the beginning of my sales career, the company I was working for sent me on a five-day intensive sales training course. It was great, but I've always referred to it as both the best and the worst sales training that I've ever received.

The content was excellent and the trainer was fabulous – there really was very little to find fault with. On paper it really was the best sales training I've ever been given. So why do I also class it as the worst? Because its overall effect on my career was the complete opposite of what it was actually intended to achieve.

When I got back on the road, I ended up being less successful, actually selling fewer boxes, than before they'd sent me on the training.

Why? Well, I was so worried about maintaining the perfect call structure, remembering all the different types of questions, accurately overcoming each type of objection and then moving on to my cleverly formulated closes that I completely lost sight of the piece of the sales jigsaw that involved me being... me!

There was nothing natural about the way I acted; I completely lost any individuality, and I became far more self-conscious and nervous.

On top of that, I wasn't focusing on the customer at all. I was trying instead to remember the role plays that I'd performed on the course and which page I should be up to with regard to my sales technique.

It's a bit like when you first learn to ride a bicycle. I bet you still remember the exact moment – that sunny afternoon years ago – when the person teaching you to ride on two wheels for the first time stopped propping you up, let go of the back of your seat and allowed you to ride off down a dusty track, as you were kept upright solely by your own balance, energy and self-belief.

When you set off on your own for that very first time, you were simply concentrating on staying upright on two wheels and avoiding hurting yourself or falling off, rather than on where you were trying to get to.

But as time went by, that focus changed and eventually you almost forgot about the bicycle underneath you, giving a lot more thought to the destination – the cycling bit just happened while you thought about other things.

Selling is all about understanding your product or service inside-out and upside-down, becoming an expert in how to effectively communicate that information, and then absorbing all that knowledge and know-how to the point of almost forgetting about it – just as you did when you eventually learnt to ride your bike properly and focused on the destination. In this case, though, you end up focusing wholly on the customer.

Just as a musician needs to concentrate completely on delivering an electrifying performance to the audience once they have absorbed the detail, depth and emotion of the music, a salesperson should be completely focused on the customer, while being able to tap unconsciously into the myriad of resources and techniques that they have stored away in their sales toolbox.

I decided to start this chapter with that analogy because questioning techniques are the most discussed sales topic of them all. And yet it's also the second most likely bit of sales advice to be casually disregarded (after "Earn the right") by thrusty young salespeople because:
a) most people believe they've heard it all before
b) few commentators ever give it the depth of focus it truly deserves.

We're all told the types of questions to ask; we're all reminded of the power that they can have over our potential customers and we're all given a roadmap to guide customers through so that they'll end up where we want to take them.

Why?

Why do we bog down junior salespeople with so much structure and confine them to such tight spaces of investigation? If all you are thinking about is which clever question to ask, how will you ever make use of the answers? If you already know where the conversation is going, why not just make your presentation and be done with it?

As a result, we have a generation of salespeople who are riding the question bicycle without giving any thought to the destination.

Why are you asking questions if you already know the answers?

Why do you ask questions that help neither you nor your client?

If all you want to do is ask questions because it's the polite thing to do before you get down to selling the only option you have in your bag, why bother? Why not just tell me?

In his book *The 7 Habits of Highly Effective People*, Stephen R. Covey discusses the importance of **seeking first to understand and then to be understood**.

As Selling with EASE moves into the bottom half of its cycle, we arrive at **Ask the appropriate questions**, followed by **Solve the problem**. As you can see from the diagram, both are underpinned by the **UNDERSTANDING** half of the process.

We're going to ask exceptional questions so that we can fully understand the customer's problem, which will uncover the opportunity for how we can help. This quarter is all about salespeople completely understanding the customer – there will be plenty of time to present and explain our solution in the next quadrant.

Seek first to understand and – only after that – to be understood.

At this point we're not going to sell anything AT the customer; we're only going to focus on the things that we don't know and ask questions so that we can find out. As discussed earlier, the customer who walks into a DIY store to buy a drill doesn't really want a drill – he wants a hole. A bad salesperson will present the drills that are on offer; a good salesperson will discuss the DIY plans with the customer. The ability to ask great questions enables us to enquire about that hole and supply the appropriate drill.

The Skill We Lost
When We Were Kids

All kids are great at asking questions, but somewhere along the way polite society and the process of becoming a grown-up knock a bit of that natural inquisitiveness out of everyone.

If you need some proof: I can almost guarantee that, in a store not too far away from where you're sitting right now, a parent and a small child are having this exact conversation.

Child: "Can I have some sweets?"
Parent: "Not now."
Child: "When?"
Parent: "After you've had your meal."
Child: "What can I have?"
Parent: "Some of your favourites."
Child: "How many can I have?"
Parent: "One packet."
Child: "Can I have two?"
Parent: "No"
Child: "Why not?"
Parent: "Because I said so."
Child: "Why?"
Parent: "Just be glad you're getting something."
Child: "I am, but why can I only have one?"

Without realising it, that child is almost exclusively asking **open questions**, all demanding answers that will deliver information and moving the conversation towards the child's desired outcome. In between those wonderful open questions, there are a couple of **closed questions** used to obtain confirmation and gain commitment.

I guess it's hardly surprising that, faced with this kind of clever, relentless questioning every day, our elders found a variety of ways to ensure that our inquisitiveness slowly diminished over time.

But that's such a massive shame. We appear to have been blessed with this skill right at the beginning of our life, only for it to be slowly diluted – and sometimes completely erased – simply because those we questioned were too exhausted to supply us with the answers that we never stopped pestering them for.

The Two Most Important Questions in the Whole World

Once again, please don't skip this just because it looks too basic for you – there are nuggets of information in the next few pages that people pay good money to make sure they completely understand.

In many books this subject is oversimplified and glossed over, assuming that we all know how to ask great questions, or it becomes bogged down with multi-layered theories and boring, lengthy scripts.

My aim is to be somewhere in between: I'm going to tackle the subject in-depth, while doing my very best to keep it all as simple as possible. We're going to put together the *"question jigsaw"* piece by piece, introducing all the different elements one at a time, step by step, until we've created a scene which everyone can relate to and understand.

Of course, as with any picture puzzle, we need to find a recognisable starting point, such as the ground and the sky, the corners or outer edges - some kind of helpful framework – a foundation stone on which to build. This comes in the form of the first two – and most important – categories:

- open questions
- closed questions.

Most people will hear about them at the beginning of their sales career, decide that they've got them perfected after a brief explanation and then go on to request something a bit more *advanced*.

But that really doesn't do them the justice they deserve. "Open" and "closed" are the two hinges on which the heavy doors of questioning hang and operate.

These two types of questions permeate through every questioning strategy known to man. They are the Rosetta Stone of sales technique. Every other kind of question – however cleverly titled or thought out – can always be classed as either an open question or a closed question.

And that is why they sit proudly at the centre of this **questioning skills** diagram.

Open Questions

The clue with open questions is in their name: they are used to 'OPEN UP' the conversation, by enabling customers to deliver information that will help us to help them, and to give a platform on which to discuss in detail the things that really matter.

On the whole, they mostly start with one of these six words:

Who What Where When Why How

If you ask an open question, your customer should never be able to answer with just a YES or a NO – that is how you will know if you're asking true open questions or not.

As an example, if you were to ask your friend:

"Are you going to France this summer?" or *"Is Bob going to the concert with you?"*

They could easily answer with a yes or a no.

However, if you were to ask:

"Where are you spending your next vacation?" or *"Who are you going to the concert with?"*

They would have to give you a more detailed response.

In the same way, you can't just answer the questions below with a yes or a no.

*"**Who** gave you your first kiss?"*
*"**What** do you weigh?"*
*"**Where** has all your hair gone?"*
*"**When** are you going to grow up?"*
*"**Why** does this keep happening to me?"*
*"**How** much is that doggy in the window?"*

Although most open questions start with these six words, there are a few other ways to phrase a question so that you'll receive more than just a yes or a no answer.

One more word particularly stands out. For instance, *"**Which** wine would you like to drink tonight?"* would require some form of detailed response.

Portuguese Raindrops

As sales professionals, we're supposed to be fabulous at asking great questions and finding out what customers really want – unfortunately, over the years I have come across the complete opposite.

The realisation of what the main problem is dawned on me at a foundation sales training workshop a couple of years ago and it reminded me of something.

Indulge me while I share a holiday memory...

We'd just landed in Portugal – it was Easter time, back before we had children – I was walking with my (now) wife and, after dropping the bags off at our apartment, we went for a short walk to the little grocery store to stock up on a few essentials. On the way back, carrying a stick of bread and a few bottles of wine, it suddenly started raining.

But these weren't little raindrops like we get back at home – oh no! – it was as if kids were standing on a nearby rooftop dropping water bombs that were landing around us and crashing to the ground. Every single raindrop was huge, and I mean *massive*. And, while my wife sensibly took cover under a tree, I just stood in the downpour – amazed.

I'm from the North of England so I'm used to a bit of rain – but this was awesome. These weren't inconsequential pitter-patter raindrops, falling like tiny diamonds from the sky; every one of those huge balls of water seemed to fall and hit the ground like huge goldfish bowls of water. And I was as mesmerised as a baby witnessing falling snow for the very first time.

That memory came rushing back to me while training a group of young salespeople not too long ago; I was asking delegates to formulate a few open questions that would help them to get to the very heart of what their customers really needed.

Their responses only scratched at the edge of every problem. They were asking little *peck, peck, peck* questions – tiny pitter-patter raindrop questions. In fact, if the effectiveness of any one of those questions could have somehow been measured like rainfall, no one would have even realised that the weather had changed.

What they needed were big, bold drown-me-in-the-enormity-of-it-all questions.

Questions that really got people racking their brain and which could really catapult us into long, meaningful conversations. Questions that, when asked, could keep someone talking for hours.

Here's a strange fact about brilliant questions: the shorter they are, the longer the corresponding answer.

If we haven't put any thought into what we might be asking until we're actually sitting in front of the customer, we stretch out our questions in an effort to give them relevance and meaning, and to make them a little more understandable.

On the other hand, well-thought-out great, big raindrop questions are constructed to be simple and direct. These questions enable us to spend all our time understanding the customer, as opposed to the customer trying to work out what we're actually asking.

Here's an example of a biggie:

"What are the three most important things that you want every member of your team to be able to achieve next year?"

SPLASH!

Here's another:

"What's currently holding them back from achieving those three things?"

SPLOSH!

Scan through the next page and see if you can find a few big raindrop questions that you can use during the preparations for your next sales appointment or call; they could also be a foundation to create some of your own.

30 Big Open Questions

What difference do you want to see?
What do you like about your current supplier?
What size budget are we working with?
What do you most want to see happen?
What other points are important to you?

What is your top priority?
What reservations do you have?
What is stopping you from changing this?
This is how I see it – what am I missing?
What bit of this is really important to you?
If you could change three things, what would they be?
What's holding you back from reaching your goals?

Who will benefit most?
Who needs to be involved in the process?
Who do you want this to be seen by?
Who won't like this?

When do you need this by?
When do you want to start seeing results?

How many people are involved?
How do you see it working?
How will you measure its success?
How do you want this to be remembered?

How long have we got before it's too late?

How can I help you to get this right?
How do we make this better than…?
How do you think senior management are going to evaluate
the success of this initiative?

Where do you see this fitting in?
Where do you see the situation in 12 months?

Why do you think that keeps happening?
Why are you looking to change?

Becoming Consultative

Lots of people have written about consultative selling – in fact, you can read entire books on the technique if you wish to.

In an effort to demystify the subject, I've dedicated the next couple of pages to explaining why adopting a consultative approach can ensure that you're another few steps ahead of the regular sales crowd.

Imagine for a moment that when you visit your doctor – after you've said hello and pulled up a chair – they immediately push a small container of pills towards you and say:

"Take two of those three times a day!"

Slightly bewildered, you might question the fact that the doctor has no idea what's wrong with you, to which they reply:

"I know, but that dosage usually sorts out most of my patients' problems 90% of the time!"

You mention that you're not happy but the reply is a shrug followed by:

"You can go and get a second opinion if you want, but the recommendation will probably be the same, so you might as

well just start taking the pills now and get the problem sorted."

Clearly, that wouldn't be acceptable – in fact, you'd have every right to be terribly upset – and yet that's how many salespeople present their product or service every day: only moments after a "hello" and a handshake they've already started presenting what they've come in to sell you.

Consultative selling is a phrase that was first mooted decades ago – and yet nearly half a century after the event, we're all still dealing with salespeople who are more interested in selling **AT** us, rather than finding out what we need and then matching what they have to our requirements.

Funnily enough, the questions you'd want to be asked by your doctor really don't differ greatly from the questions that your customers would like to hear from you.

- *Where does it hurt?*
- *What negative effects has this been having on your normal standard of life?*
- *How long have you been feeling like this?*
- *What happened that made you decide to get it sorted out?*
- *How soon would you like to go ahead with the solution?*
- *Who else needs to be informed?*
- *What extra support do you need?*

Tweak two or three of those and you'll probably find out more about your next customer than you thought they'd ever tell you. Now, you might think that this approach won't work within your particular industry – and that may be true – if you've ever been to see a doctor who wasn't even slightly interested in you as an individual then you'll probably have a fair idea of how all your customers feel about dealing with you at this moment in time.

Taking a genuine interest in other people isn't really a sales skill – it's what decent, polite human beings do when someone has a problem that they can't solve by themselves.

Think about this for a moment: asking for help means lowering your defences and making yourself quite vulnerable. Neither of these comes naturally when you're in the same room as someone trying to sell you something. It's when we need to feel that we're being fully listened to with empathy and a higher level of understanding.

Becoming consultative – whether you think you need to or not – might not get the job done any quicker, but it will almost certainly increase the number of customers who decide to work with you more than just the once.

The House Game

If you've participated in any form of group sales training with me over recent years, you will almost certainly have played The House Game.

Essentially, everyone pairs up and then sits back-to-back. One individual has a blank sheet of paper and a pencil, while the other holds a simple sketch of a house, hidden from the eyes of their partner. The person holding the pencil is given five minutes to extract enough relevant information, using only open questions, to draw the house without ever seeing it.

Although it sounds simple enough, it never takes long for the exercise to turn into a barrage of guesses and stabs in the dark – random ideas of what the house might look like.

The questions change from open questions – those that uncover information regarding the actual picture – into questions that simply seek clarification of the version of the house that they have pictured in their mind.

For example, instead of asking: *"What's on the roof?"* they ask *"Is there a chimney?"*

Instead of asking: *"What's outside?"* they ask *"Is there a garden?"*

And instead of asking: *"What kind of house is it?"* they ask *"Are there two floors?"*

As consultative as we might think we are sometimes, we often walk in to see our customers and prospects with a picture already set in our minds. We know what we have to sell, we know what this kind of customer normally buys and we know how long we've got to do it all in.

That's why we tend to ask so many questions even though we already know the answers. It helps us to feel like we're in control, as we steer the customer towards the destination we were always trying to take them to.

Unfortunately, your customer won't feel like you're really very interested in their problem at all. They don't want your version of their dream scenario; they want you to come in and sketch THEIR version of their dream scenario – and then help them to achieve it.

Your customers are (desperately) waiting for someone to truly hear what they say and fully understand it.

As far as they're concerned, there is a constant line of salespeople who walk in with a series of boxes to sell: they feel the need to make pointless small talk, while feigning interest, before clumsily moving towards their close. Most people think that they're great at asking questions – but are you asking those questions to uncover the truth so that you can help or are you just going through the motions so that you can get to the order?

Clearly, I know that getting the order is important; I know that's the objective of the entire call, but ask yourself this: do you regularly decide what you're going to sell to someone before you even start the conversation?

Is all this questioning and small talk just for show?

Imagine a police artist asking the witness of a crime to describe who they saw at the scene, so that a detailed sketch of the suspect could be drawn. Would the police artist be regarded as effective if all the portraits were exceptional, gallery-quality pictures but absolutely none of them looked anything like the criminals at large?

No, of course they wouldn't, because that's not their job; their role is to create a likeness so that the witness will be able to point at it and say:

"Yes! That's him! That's the man!"

In the same way, if you held up your notes at the end of your sales appointments, would your customers recognise their problems, hopes and dreams? Would they feel that somebody really understood them?

They should be able to point at your notes and say:

"Yes! That's it! That's my problem!"

Walking in with no concrete presumptions and gaining a deep enough understanding to draw the picture that is in your customer's mind – followed by even deeper questions to correct every detail until your version matches their vision – are some of the hardest sales skills to master. However, once you have, you will experience one of the greatest feelings of job satisfaction that you've ever felt – and it's a heck of a lot easier to achieve if you know how to ask great big open questions rather than just hoping, guessing and simply stabbing in the dark.

Closed Questions

Essentially, a closed question is any question which doesn't start with Who, What, Why, Where, When and How (and, on some occasions, which).

Whenever you are asked a closed question, if you don't feel very chatty, you can just answer with a yes or a no.

That's quite simplistic, though: most people tend to deliver a lot more information than that when asked, but with an open question you can guarantee some form of detailed response whereas with closed questions you can't.

For instance, if I asked you the following questions, you wouldn't necessarily have to give much of an answer – other than "yes" or "no".

"Do you have a dog?"

"Does your house have a cellar?"

"Have you had any problems with the neighbours?"

"Are you concerned about aliens?"

"Is the problem something I can help with?"

However, it's important to realise that just because the answers you receive from closed questions are short and to the point, it doesn't make them the evil twin of open questions.

Indeed, at certain times being able to limit the range of a customer's response to a simple choice of one or the other, yes or no, can be extremely useful.

- **Closed questions can help to uncover opportunities**. Sometimes customers can be extremely guarded around salespeople – after all, allowing you to know how much pain they are *really* in might mean that you will take advantage of them somehow. So, rather unhelpfully (for you and them), they keep their wants, needs and problems close to their chest. There are also instances when they actually don't know what they need or don't even realise that they have a problem. Closed questions can be extremely useful at times like this, when you're trying to find out if there is a genuine opportunity for you to help.

Here are a couple of examples.

"Are you happy with the profit margin you make when you sell that brand...?"

"One of my customers told me recently that this happened. Has that ever been a problem for you?"

- **Closed questions can help to confirm needs**. Sometimes customers will happily throw an opportunity into the conversation, but not everything that sounds like an opportunity to the salesperson is necessarily a genuine problem that the customer needs solving. When they mention something that might be classed as an opportunity, you should ask questions to confirm whether or not they actually want that problem to be solved. Otherwise, you could end up like the Boy Scout who keeps helping old people across the road, whether they want to go or not.

Here are a couple of examples.

"Is that hole in the roof starting to get on your nerves?"

"Is that something you want to change?"

- **Closed questions can help to gain commitment**. Just as open questions are used to open up the conversation, closed questions can be used to close it. For all the mystery and magic that is spun around the art of closing, essentially it just boils down to someone asking a closed question that gains the other person's commitment to move forward positively.

Here are a couple of examples.

"If I process this now, you can have it by Friday – is that OK?"

"Would you like it in red or blue?"

Questions that Start out Open but End up Closed

This isn't actually a third type of question: it's just the way in which too many people seek to understand their fellow human beings without realising how much they're restricting the answer.

Think about instances when someone asked you a question that went a bit like this:

"What do you want to drink – orange juice?"

"What would you like for dinner – fish?"

"When would like to go for a swim? I'm going at 3 o'clock."

Although they mean well, they're just giving the illusion of choice. So, if you're trying to understand someone or uncover information that you currently don't know:

Give it some thought and keep it short.

Misconceptions about Questioning Techniques

Some people seem to think that OPEN questions are good and CLOSED questions are bad, but that isn't the case at all. They are just useful tools with their own place and purpose. The choice of when – and how – to use them is what can be either good or bad.

After all, using any tool inappropriately can cause you problems; just as you wouldn't use a screwdriver to bang in a nail, you wouldn't use a closed question to uncover detailed information.

Also, an overuse of any type of question, open or closed, will present difficulties.

If all you have are questions, questions and more questions, the following problems are bound to occur.

- **Your customer will switch off**. There is a limit to the number of queries that a customer can put up with. If you are going to ask a series of questions one after the other, the likelihood is that their responses will just get shorter and shorter as the interrogation continues. Also, if they can't see an objective or end point, they are going to start wondering about the purpose of all these queries – and soon they'll just get bored and ask you to leave.

- **Your customer will become defensive**. Since they know that you are trying to sell them something, they are already quite cautious, so if you just go in with question after question, designed to get you what you want rather than helping them, then the conversation will run the risk of suffocating under the relentless, desperate quest for small facts. They are already being careful with their choice of words in case you trap them with your magical and mysterious salesperson ways. If you question them into a corner, they will just refuse to continue. You're not a sheepdog herding a rogue lamb back to its pen. Give them a little psychological breathing space and let them relax.

Remember: asking questions isn't the objective.

When you are trying to sell something or increase business somehow, questions won't get the order by themselves – a couple of answers would really help, too.

So how do we use open and closed questions effectively, without scaring the life out of the customer?

We introduce some verbal **CUES**.

Labelling Your Next Conversation

It's always difficult to change and improve a process if it's only ever referred simply as *"The Process"*. However, once you've broken it down, you begin to realise that all the parts aren't as equally effective. When you start to identify and label each of those separate pieces, you can work out how effective they are in achieving your goal.

Understanding what they are and what they do enables you to focus on reducing the things that have a negative or neutral impact, while increasing the factors which have the most positive influence on your desired outcome.

With that in mind, there are two more groups of questions that I want to introduce but, before I do that, I want to be very clear about a couple of things.

Both sets of questions are part of a framework, a toolbox in which to dip in and out. They are definitely not rigid step-by-step questioning techniques built to confine and restrict you during a conversation.

If your focus is on asking the next *right* question, rather than helping the customer to make a great buying decision, then the link between the two of you will begin to deteriorate very quickly indeed.

So here's a strange request:

Please don't try to use any of the questions analysed in the next few pages during any of your sales calls for at least a month after reading this chapter.

Just become aware of their existence and label them. Learn what they are and how to use them in your own way. You're probably using some of them already without knowing it but, since the process is only ever generally referred to as "*Questioning*", you never get a chance to break it down or improve it.

So over the next four weeks, listen to the questions that you are asking your customers, categorise them and recognise what effect they have on – and where they take – the conversation.

You'll be amazed at how quickly your results will improve, once you realise the impact that some of your current questions are having on your success and start making the necessary adjustments.

We All Need Verbal CUES

Surrounding open and closed questions on the questioning skills diagram, we are now going to add four sub-categories:
• **Context**
• **Understanding**
• **Effect**
• **Solution.**

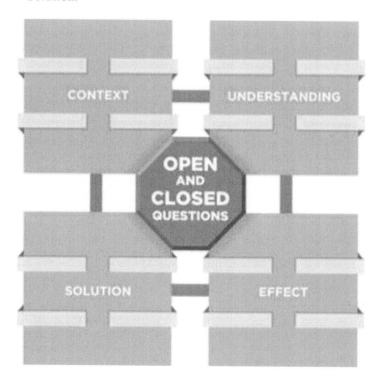

Context Questions

Context questions generally sound more like friendly chatter than business talk. In fact, they are the sort of things you would ask an old school friend if you met up after some years. For example:

"How have you been?"

"What do you do for a job now?"

"Do you have any kids?"

They put things into context. They frame the next part of the conversation and allow us to put the edges of the jigsaw in place so that we have a better understanding of the picture as a whole.

If you were making a sales call, they'd sound something like:

"What does your company produce?"

"How many people work at this factory?"

"How's business going?"

Context questions can be incredibly useful and serve as wonderful icebreakers, but it's important to realise that they can easily annoy your customers.

According to an old sales adage, everybody's favourite subject is themselves – people just love talking about themselves. There is some truth in that, but let's look at this realistically. If you've just called me on the phone or booked an appointment to come in and see me, I have to make time in my day to speak with you.

I'm not just sitting around, wishing for somebody to come in and talk to me; I'm busy, busy, busy. The activities taking up my time are already expanding to a point so far away in the distance that I can no longer see the last thing on my to-do list. I really don't need anyone or anything to make that situation worse.

When you're running a business, everyone who walks into your office is there for one of the following three reasons:
- to help
- to become a customer
- to get in the way.

If you ask too many context questions, your customer will eventually start to wonder which one of those categories you actually belong to.

In this day and age customers will very quickly start to ponder why, with all the wisdom of the world only a mouse click away, the person in front of them hasn't even bothered to look up the most basic information about them.

Think hard about the context questions you use on a regular basis: are they making you look professional and friendly or uninformed and ineffective?

Understanding Questions

These are the questions that you use when you want to start drawing the picture of the house that's in your customer's mind. They help the customer to tell you about problems they might be experiencing or what they think they need to realise their hopes, dreams, goals and targets. Understanding questions include things like:

"What do you most want to see happen?"
"If you could change three things, what would they be?"

"How can I help you to get this right?"

"Why are you looking to change?"

Effect Questions

Once you've drawn such a detailed and accurate picture that your customer can point to it and say: *"That's it! That's my problem!"* you can move on to uncovering the true value of the solution.

Effect questions require answers that uncover the consequences of not solving the problem or receiving a substandard solution. They are the questions that focus the customer on making the right decision.

You'll recognise that you have asked an effect question when the answer feels quite negative; in a business situation they might include the following:

"What will happen if you let this situation continue?"

"What do the Directors think about the problem?"

"How is this affecting staff morale?"

"How much business is at stake if this project fails?"

Effect questions are incredibly powerful tools; they force the customer to confront the reality of the situation and to verbalise the importance of getting things right. However, for this reason, they can be quite difficult to ask. In fact, most salespeople would rather not ask questions that introduce an element of negativity into their sales presentations – and who can blame them.

However, don't shy away from them altogether, but use them with care – and once you have used an effect question, make sure that you're ready to ask a question belonging to the next category to lighten the mood.

Solution Questions

Solution questions help to focus the customer back onto how you can help and start a positive conversation in which they talk to you about a future that involves your product or service. Put simply, the emphasis should return to the good things that are going to happen and all the benefits of making a great buying decision.

Solution questions are easy to ask because everybody likes the answer. When following on from an effect question, they are more likely to be of the closed variety, as you'll be looking for a form of commitment from the customer rather than seeking any level of information. They sound a bit like these:

"So, will getting this fixed as soon as possible help?"

"If we improved staff morale, do you think productivity would improve too?"

"So, is making this run smoothly from start to finish important to you?"

"Putting an end to those worries and sleepless nights will make a huge difference, won't it?"

Some words of advice before we move on: using solution questions in isolation or introducing them too early into your sales presentation will make them sound just like one of those elevator speeches I discussed earlier and despise so much.

Without **context**, **understanding** and **effect** questions, you'll end up sounding just like a really bad radio commercial. You know the kind of thing: *"Hi, if your carpet could be cleaned in just 50% of the time, with an improvement in noticeable cleanliness of more than 200%, wouldn't that be just great?!"*

Also, it's probably not a great idea to introduce an effect or solution question if you don't have the ability to solve the problem being discussed – doing so will actually decrease your perceived value with the customer rather than adding to it.

Now OVER-achieve with Four More Questions

We're now going to lay an extra layer of questions **OVER** the **CUES** quadrants. **OVER questions** can be found in the carefully prepared sales presentations of every successful salesperson, but due to the subtlety of their impact and effect, it's quite difficult to recognise when they're actually in play.

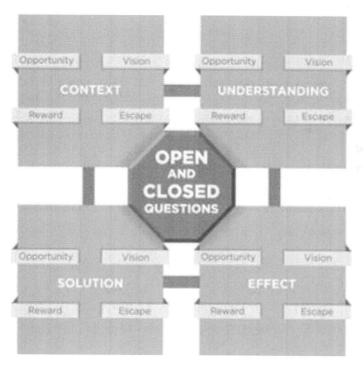

OVER stands for:
• **O**pportunity
• **V**ision
• **E**scape
• **R**eward.

These questions are interwoven with each of the four CUES quadrants, helping you to get an even better understanding of your customer's real needs and enabling them to independently recognise the true value of your proposal.

They also help to draw out any objections nice and early, so you can deal with them and then concentrate on helping the customer to make a great buying decision.

Prepare yourself with just one question from each category and I guarantee you'll uncover more useful information than 90% of your competition ever do – and your customer will feel that someone is genuinely interested in their problem rather than just turning up to flog them the next new gizmo. In order to make them completely clear, I'll explain the OVER questions one at a time and give you a few examples of how they help to get the most out of each quadrant.

Opportunity

These questions are used to uncover the business opportunities for you and your company. They live mostly in the Context and Understanding quadrants, as they're employed to find out how you can help and how much assistance the customer is going to need. Do your homework first to keep these down to a minimum, but not at the expense of understanding the opportunity in full.

Examples

Context: *"How many people will require these new machines?"*

Understanding: *"What kind of things do you want the machines to do for you?"*

Effect: *"Will a lengthy lead time cause you problems?"*

Solution: *"How soon will you need them?"*

Vision

These questions are used to flesh out the customer's vision, i.e. what they want the future to look like. Your vision questions will create the detailed drawing – the exact house – that your customer is thinking of. Vision questions are found throughout the four CUES quadrants, as they help to explain why the meeting is happening in the first place.

Examples

Context: *"What system do you have running at the moment?"*

Understanding: *"What system would you like to have?"*

Effect: *"What happens when your current system becomes obsolete?"*

Solution: *"Would having a system that eradicates those concerns be the kind of thing you're looking for?"*

Escape

Escape questions should be used to discover the current pain or uncomfortable consequences that the customer is trying to get away from. What is the buyer personally trying to avoid? What are the consequences to them as an individual if this is allowed to continue?

Examples

Context: *"When did you first start realising there was a problem?"*

Understanding: *"What knock-on effects have those problems caused?"*

Effect: *"What happens if we don't do something about it?"*

Solution: *"Do you want to make sure this never happens again?"*

Reward

The reward questions uncover the benefits that they'll enjoy for making a positive change. In a similar vein to Escape questions, they can be personal, according to how the buyer will profit from organising the perfect solution.

Examples

Context: *"Who wants this change to happen?"*

Understanding: *"How will they feel when you get it all sorted out?"*

Effect: *"What will they say to you if the solution doesn't work properly?"*

Solution: *"If they saw results like these, would that make them happy?"*

The Most Important Sales Technique that No One Ever Talks About

Questioning techniques are all well and good, but if you don't understand that there are as many rules to listening as there are to asking, you will miss out on loads of stuff.

If you want to get the sales that others simply never even realised existed, the answer lies in what I like to call deep listening, and the best way to describe this is with the Chinese symbol for the verb "*to listen*", which essentially reads:

"I give you my ears, my eyes,
my undivided attention and my heart."

This is just about the best definition for listening that I've ever come across.

Most salespeople ask questions for the sake of asking questions; they rarely hear the answers. Others never stop talking long enough to warrant a response.

I know we've just spent an entire chapter talking about how to ask the most appropriate questions, but it's all a bit pointless if you don't listen to the answers in their entirety – words, inflexion and underlying meaning.

Listening is all about being there at that moment in time. It isn't checking your watch because you have three more calls to do or staring around at the other people in the room while the customer is talking. It's about showing respect and taking an interest.
If the customer has given up their time to see you, don't blow it because your attention span doesn't stretch far enough to finding out how you can actually help.

Ten Essential Rules to Deep Listening

- First of all, listen to fully understand and then respond – and only in that order. If you didn't understand, say so and ask again.
- Don't spend the time when a customer is responding to your question, or trying to tell you something, thinking of your next question.
- If you have already made up your mind what the answer is going to be, why ask? Alternatively, ask, listen and learn.

- There will be a point when you become conscious that you stopped listening; tune back into the conversation. If you think you missed something important, politely find a way of getting them to go over the information.
- Don't interrupt – even if you're really excited. It's still rude.
- Keep eye contact as much as you can (without being spooky) and react accordingly with appropriate listening sounds and facial expressions.
- Qualify what you have heard, e.g. "So if I heard you right, you are saying that…"
- Two ears and one mouth – use them (as often as possible) in that ratio.
- You are not always right. Their opinion matters, so give them a chance to tell you everything – absolutely everything – that they so desperately want to get off their chest.
- Make notes or put your hands down – don't fidget.

"Our survey demonstrates that 90% of Purchasing Managers fail to grasp how desperately they need our product."

4 | SOLVE THE PROBLEM

Helping the Customer to Understand Why You're the Best Person for the Job

Quadrant three continues round through the UNDERSTANDING half of the cycle, but it's at this point that the focus turns away from recognising the requirements of the customer and moves on towards helping them to grasp how you propose to make a difference.

Once you've diagnosed the problem, you need to know what you have within your portfolio that will deliver the customer's desired outcome; that's when you will require a whole new toolbox of skills to ensure that your message is presented as professionally – and received as effectively – as possible.

This isn't just about learning how to stand in front of a 50-slide presentation designed six months ago by your marketing team. Of course, getting the information across is important, but you also need to be able to communicate with different personality types, recognise their buying motives and overcome their objections.

You Probably Have More Answers than You Think

Have you ever heard of the Portuguese word *saudade*?

Surprisingly, it has no direct translation into English; it describes a distinct sense of longing for something that doesn't actually exist.

It's used a lot in poetry and music to describe an "*emptiness*" – like someone or something that should be there but is missing; *saudade* is an absence that you can feel.

You'll find that many of your prospects and customers are suffering from a form of *saudade* that they can't cure themselves because they have no idea that a remedy exists. Nowadays, they can find almost everything they want with a simple click of the mouse, but how would they go about finding something that doesn't exist? Where would they start searching and why would they even try to in the first place?

Sometimes when we walk in to see prospects and customers, it's too easy to believe that they're as clued-up about our area of expertise as we are but, more often than not, that can be far from the truth.

Simply put: "*People don't know what they don't know*" – how could they? Customers might be experts in their own field, but normally our products or services only account for a fraction of what they spend their time and efforts working on during the year, which is why they require our help.

The best explanation I've found to describe the statement above comes in the form a story, which I originally heard told by Bryan Williams.

A guy goes out to his car only to find that the front right tyre had been stolen... completely gone!

So he puts the spare wheel on and drives to the garage. After explaining what has happened to the attendant, he proceeds to order a new tyre. The attendant obliges and tells him that it will arrive the following day.

On his way out, the manager stops him and asks if he got everything he needed. After telling him yes, he also tells him about the wheel mishap and the manager asks:

"So you've ordered the wheel locks, right?"

The customer has never heard of a wheel lock, so the manager explains that it prevents tyres from being stolen, and he should consider ordering some.

Of course he should – that's a great idea! If he'd had them this morning none of this would have happened. On his way out he goes to see the attendant that took the order and asks: "Why didn't you recommend the wheel locks?"

"You never asked about them," replies the attendant.

Whether you know it or not, your customers feel this *saudade* all the time. It's the sensation we all get when something isn't quite right but we don't know what would make it better – just a distinct sense of longing for something that doesn't appear to exist. No amount of searching on the internet or meetings with colleagues can deliver the answer because they don't even know what they're looking for.

Once you've uncovered the customer's problems and understood their vision, the answer might appear incredibly obvious to you, but it might not be to everyone else.

You are the solution to your customer's *saudade*; just because they don't recognise it yet should never put you off. After all, nobody wants to walk out and find their front tyre missing, do they?

Give Your Customers a Personality Test

One of the most important skills you can have in your toolbox as a sales professional is the ability to help the people who need your expertise, recognise that you are the best person to solve their problems.

In order to be able to do that, it's important to remember that absolutely everyone is in some way different; indeed, even the most identical of twins have their own unique personalities and set of fingerprints. Therefore, selling to the world with our *"everyone's the same"* blinkers on would mean failing to fully understand the needs of certain groups and individuals.

But even worse than that, if we only understand how to serve a small section of our potential audience, surely that means that some people might not respond well or completely fail to understand the message we are trying to get across. Maybe some would feel intimidated by a direct sales approach, whereas others might get annoyed if it wasn't direct enough.

So how do we make sure that we're presenting the right words, in the right way, to the right people – all of the time?

Well, in an effort to understand ourselves and others better, we can take a look at the work of Carl Gustav Jung, a Swiss psychiatrist and psychotherapist who pioneered analytical psychology.

He recognised that there is a huge difference in the way people respond to different situations. In fact, we have Jung to thank for devising the words **extrovert** – from the Latin words *extra*, meaning "out", and *vertere*, meaning "to turn" – and **introvert** (where *intro* comes from the Latin word for "inward").

Armed with this knowledge, it doesn't take a genius to realise that strongly orientated extroverts and introverts see things in completely different ways, which can easily, and quite often, cause conflict and misunderstandings.

Jung's book *Psychological Types*, published in 1921, also paved the way for what became the Myers-Briggs Type Indicator tests, which most people have probably encountered at one time or another, typically during the application process for a new job.

In order to help you see how the preferences of certain personality types can differ enormously when they find themselves cornered by a well-meaning salesperson, I'd like to take you through an extremely crude version of one of these tests.

In the diagram, you will see the numbers one to ten running across the horizontal axis, which is bracketed by the words "Extrovert" and "Introvert". In the same way, straight down the middle on the vertical axis, the numbers run up from one to ten. At the bottom of the scale is "Fact" and at the top "Feeling".

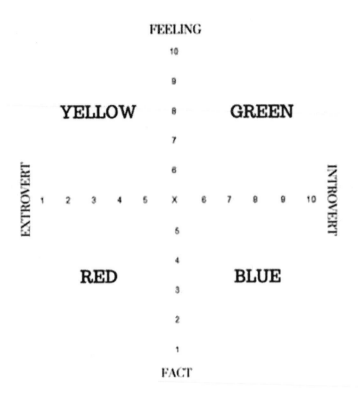

In each of the quadrants there is the name of a colour: yellow, green, blue and red.

Take a couple of minutes and have a think about how those closest to you – the people who know you best – would reply if they were asked to follow these next three steps on your behalf.

Step One – Introvert or Extrovert

The thought of attending a social gathering or event can delight some people, while others would start practising their excuses for not being able to make it as soon as the invitation was delivered.

Some would be happy to ride naked through town on the back of a white charger only wearing a party hat, whereas others would prefer to hide in the back of a cupboard, wearing a heavy-knit jumper and a balaclava.

Would the people who know you best say that at a party you are happy to chat and mingle? (If so, mark yourself somewhere between one and five, with one being the most extrovert.) Or would they say that the thought of making small talk and having to spend the evening with strangers fills you with dread? (If so, mark yourself somewhere between six and ten, with ten being the most introvert.)

Step Two – Fact or Feeling

There are some people who are deeply into detail: they love paperwork and can focus in a studious manner at the drop of the hat. Just for the record, I'm not one of them.

Certain people see the words *"Have you read the terms and conditions of this website?"* and will proceed to examine every single one of them, before venturing another click further. Others, however, will happily tap on the "Continue" button, blissfully unaware of what they have just agreed to.

Some of your friends will tell you that they made a recent decision because it just felt right, whereas others took months to come to a conclusion one way or the other.

Step two is much harder to quantify than step one, but if I were to ask your friends whether you make most of your decisions with you head or your heart, what would they say?

So, step two: on the vertical axis of the diagram put a circle around a number – one to ten – as to where you think the people who know you best would mark you on this scale. One to five, with your head, or six to ten, with your heart?

Step Three – In Which Quadrant Do They Cross?

So, for example, if you marked yourself as a three on the horizontal (extrovert) and eight on the vertical (feeling) and then drew two lines to see where they crossed, you would find yourself in the yellow quadrant.

Alternatively, if you marked yourself as an eight on the horizontal (introvert) and three on the vertical (fact), and then drew two lines to see where they crossed, you would find yourself in the blue quadrant. Which is your quadrant? Whichever one it is, mark it with a cross.

So why does this matter? Well, everybody seems to be aware of the saying:

"You should treat others the way YOU expect to be treated yourself."

Quite right, you certainly should: it's a fabulous place to start. However, as we've just discovered, at least 75% of the population aren't even the in same personality quadrant as you, so if you think about it, that wouldn't be very effective.

Also, however noble and well-meaning the underlying intent of this message is, you are the only YOU. Nobody else wants to be treated *exactly* the same way as you do, because there isn't another one of YOU.

Here is a different example: you couldn't take a group of teenagers whose only experience of dining out has come from eating at a fast-food burger chain and expect them to instantly become waiters at a top-end restaurant just by saying:

> *"Treat the customers the way YOU would expect to be treated yourself."*

You would quickly find that the restaurant customers have completely different expectations with regards to service than the teenagers, who have never witnessed the delivery and output of a top-end restaurant.

So maybe it would be safer to say that:

> *"We should treat other people the way that THEY expect to be treated."*

Understanding Other Personality Types

I'm aware that this isn't the most scientific personality test you'll ever take, but I'm not trying to place you accurately in your own box. What I want to do here is show you the rough space that your personality inhabits and then explain how wildly different 75% of the population is to you. By understanding this, you will be able to adapt your presentation style to accommodate their requirements.

Yellow (Expressive)

Most people who end up in the yellow quadrant find it quite easy to communicate with others. They like to tell stories based on their personal experiences and are happy to take their time building relationships.

Although they don't tend to be really big on detail, they are quite quick decision-makers. Their friends might describe them as creative and inspirational, but they can also be known as impulsive and unpredictable.

They like to feel accepted and needed, but don't really have much of a concentration span when it comes to procedure.

Green (Amiable)
Greens are really pleasant people to be around. They like to talk about their friends and family, and will quite often use words that describe feelings and emotions throughout their normal conversation.

They really don't like to be pushed, or feel that they are being pushed, into making a decision.

Their friends would say that they are supportive and dependable, but would also describe them as the type of people who find it hard to embrace change and, in certain circumstances, are easily upset.

Blue (Analytical)
The people in this quadrant don't like a lot of small talk; they tend to be thoughtful, and appreciate deep and detailed facts, figures and data.

They like to take their time when it comes to making a decision and, like the Greens, really don't appreciate being pushed. They are sticklers for punctuality and require high levels of accuracy from those who deliver any sort of information to them.

Their friends would describe them as industrious and organised, while pointing out that they can be overly critical at times and frequently indecisive.

Red (Driver)
The people in this quadrant tend to gravitate to leadership roles in all the different aspects of their life. They like things to be done quickly and are more interested in getting on with the job at hand and making sure it's done properly than they are about becoming friends with anyone involved.

Before making decisions – and they like to make decisions quickly – they expect to see some proof. Vague notions or ideas based on emotion won't cut it: they want to be presented with some facts and figures.

Their friends would describe them as strong-willed and decisive, but might also define them as dominating and unnecessarily (and unknowingly) rude.

Effectively Adapting Your Presentation Style

At the beginning of their career, salespeople spend quite a lot of their time successfully selling to those who sit firmly inside the yellow and green quadrants. This is simply because Yellows and Greens are quite easy to sell to. They don't necessarily want a lot of detail (many of their decisions are made simply because they *feel* right), and some will go ahead and buy just because they like the salesperson.

With regard to targets and commission cheques, this looks great, at least on the surface: salespeople find prospects, prospects sign on the dotted line… Happy days!

However, the ease with which those orders are acquired also tends to have a couple of negative effects on the longer-term results of many newbie salespeople (and a few seasoned professionals too). First of all, having no previous examples to measure against, they take all the credit for the new contracts, rather than facing up to the rather uncomfortable truth that, with the Yellow and Green personalities involved, the business might just as easily have been won by anyone else wearing a friendly smile and a clean shirt.

Secondly, with those successes fresh under their belt, these salespeople suddenly feel as if they were born with some kind of sales superpower, which then leads them to deduce that, since they are indeed naturally blessed with such a gift, anyone who decides not to go ahead and become a customer must surely be unreasonable, unwinnable or just plain wrong.

Therefore, every subsequent sales failure is blamed on something completely unrelated to the actions of the salesperson; everything that goes wrong must be because of an external force, something *outthere*.

This is why you will regularly hear salespeople caught in this cycle of self-delusion muttering things like:

"Our marketing material just doesn't suit customers like that."

"She said that her company only worked with scientifically proven products, so what could I do?"

"If they don't have a sense of humour, they won't appreciate my presentation style."

"Sometimes people just don't like me. I can't do anything about that."

Getting Along with Other Quadrants

If you think about it in really simple terms, it's easy to see why different types of people don't trust, or even want to spend time with, those who are at the other end of the spectrum.

• **Reds** are fact-based and extrovert – they don't want a Yellow coming in and using up precious business time by telling jokes, and they certainly haven't got space in the diary for a Green who comes in to tell them how much they care. They want action and they need to see results.

- **Blues** are also fact-based, but are introverts. So a Red selling **at** them would feel far too pushy, while the presentations from the Yellow and Green camps would appear far too light on detail.

- **Greens** are emotionally driven introverts: they want to keep everyone happy. A forceful Red would scare them to death, whereas a conversation with a Blue might make them feel emotionally distant and uncomfortable.

- **Yellows** might be emotionally driven, but they're also quite outgoing. So while they're happy to get along with almost anyone, it doesn't mean they want a Red to come in and make them feel small and stupid. Likewise, although they'll give up their time for a Blue without putting up much of a fight, to the ears of a Yellow a presentation from a Blue will sound like Eeyore (the donkey from *Winnie the Pooh*) reading a year's worth of utility bills out loud.

So it makes perfect sense to align yourself with your customer's requirements; simply adapting your presentation style within any sales scenario will have a remarkable effect on the results you achieve. By the way, I choose my words carefully here. During training workshops there are times when certain people get a little upset and think that I am asking them to somehow become chameleon-like, changing their entire personalities and becoming different people.

That's not what I'm recommending at all. I don't want you to pretend to be anyone other than wonderful, individual you. If you start pretending or acting like someone else in front of your customers, you'll find that your meetings will quickly start to become incredibly short.

I simply want you to recognise how the person sitting across the table from you wishes to receive the information you have to deliver, so that you can then adapt your presentation style accordingly.

Remember the two perceptions I mentioned in Chapter 2? Well, if you work out how to use the information below so that it works for you effectively, that's exactly what you'll achieve. This will help you to communicate with your customers in a way that leaves them feeling confident that they're dealing with a true professional: someone who can really help, who they won't mind spending their precious time with and who they can trust to get the job done.

Being Effective on the Telephone

Yellows are great chatters and have no problem with a light, humorous telephone conversation. In fact, both Yellows and Greens appreciate someone who has a warm and friendly telephone manner.

However, Blues don't want that at all. Keep it business-like and professional, and make sure that you focus on the facts, figures, dates and job at hand.

You can bet your bottom dollar that a Red will have interrupted something incredibly important to speak with you, so keep it brief and have all the information you need somewhere close at hand (if you have to go looking for your diary when you've rung up a Red to book an appointment, they will think you're an idiot).

Making Your Presentation

Yellows like to feel that they're involved, so make sure that the presentation is quite interactive and includes their input somehow. For both Yellows and Greens, the relationship with the supplier is important, so keep it friendly, and point out that you're available to answer any questions and offer advice long after you've left the building.

Blues are looking for precision and accuracy. Make sure that you discuss the processes and procedures, and can explain how you will be keeping disruptions to a minimum during the change. They want you to be exact (nothing fluffy or woolly).

Reds want to know what it will do and how it will help, and they want to look in your eyes and know that you mean what you say – so do it with conviction.

When You Need to Write to Them

If you need to write – emails, letters or proposals – a Yellow won't mind if you keep it informal, while Greens really appreciate someone who adopts a warm and friendly manner. Try to make sure that you get a couple of important points in at the beginning, though – particularly for Yellows – as trying to absorb every detail in a 100-page report will feel like swimming through treacle.

Blues don't care whether the text is long and arduous; just make sure that it's detailed and precise, with no mistakes, and that everything is cross-referenced and watertight.

On the other hand, Reds haven't got the time for something that goes on forever, so keep it short and to the point.

Helping Them All to Make a Decision

In order to make sure that the final decision leans towards you and your business, equip Yellows with testimonials from previous happy clients (they are also quite fond of promotional incentives). Greens want your word that everything will go as promised and like to feel that they will continue to receive a level of personal service that makes them feel special and appreciated.

Blues and Reds want to see a list of options, supported by proof, data and analysis.

The Things that Really Matter to Them

Yellows want to know how you're going to improve their current situation (and, by doing so, enhance their personal status and visibility within the organisation), whereas Greens are much more bothered about how it will affect other people around them and whether everyone else will like it.

If change sounds like too much effort, Yellows will always try to find an easier alternative. On the other hand, Greens will run a mile if change means having to fall out with anyone – anyone at all.

Blues want to know exactly how this solution is going to work and if your recommendations can be justified logically. Details may be the most important thing to a Blue, but remember that they are introverts at heart so be warned: a Blue will never defend a new idea internally if they don't believe they have the facts needed to save them from some form of embarrassment at a later date.

Once again, Reds want to know how your new idea is going to change things, how it's going to help and how much that help will cost. It doesn't have to be the cheapest, but it has to be affordable, tick all the boxes and deliver more value than all the other alternatives. If you want to keep a Red happy, do all that as effectively as you can in the shortest time possible.

Don't Sell the Scratch Until You Understand the Itch

Would you like to know another reason why so many salespeople fail to engage with potential customers and then end up missing out on so much business?

Let me share something with you that completely changed the way I sold things and has helped me to find success in every single sales role since.

> *Your prospects and customers do not see the commercial landscape in the same way you do – the view from their side of the desk is completely different.*

Duh! That's obvious, Chris!

Well, maybe, but that leaves you with two options: you can take that fact for granted and continue to **sell at** them or you could adopt their viewpoint and show them why it's beneficial to **buy from** you.

You probably understand the features of the products or services that you sell inside and out – and have no problems talking about them – but when you start describing them, you're taking your prospect down a presentation path that has very little to do with their own situation.

Features, Advantages and Benefits

You've probably read about "Features, Advantages and Benefits" before, but just so we're clear on definitions, I thought we'd take a look at them one at a time.

As a simple exercise during our foundation training days, we ask delegates to write this explanation next to each category.

- The Features: **what it is**.
- The Advantages: **what it does**.
- The Benefits: **how it helps**.

Virtually everything you present or discuss during a sales call will have Features; most will also have Advantages but they won't all have Benefits – and, even then, only a selection of those benefits will matter to each prospect.

Also, let me point out before we go on that each of these categories sits alone; there is no Venn diagram of Features, Advantages and Benefits.

As an example, let's take a look at a familiar household appliance: the humble kettle.

- **What it is** (Feature): it's a kettle.

- **What it does** (Advantage): it boils water effectively and efficiently, without the need to put water into a pan and onto a flame. You don't even need to watch it, because it turns itself off.

- **How it helps** (Benefit): it saves time, effort and possibly even money (with regard to energy costs). You can make a nice cup of tea without any fuss and while it's reaching the perfect temperature, you can go off and start another job without worrying that the water will boil over.

There are no crossovers there. A kettle doesn't help just because it's a kettle and although what it does might lead us to the benefits, the explanation of advantages doesn't drill down to the real reasons why we all use kettles. Yes, it's wonderful that it boils water quickly and cheaply – but that's not the benefit to us. The benefit is that when it does all those things, it saves time, money, worry and effort.

This brings us back to the point I raised in Chapter 2. If you walk into a DIY store to buy a drill, you don't want the drill: you want to make a hole. What a drill is and what it does are interesting and useful facts for drill enthusiasts, but that's not why you want to own one. What matters to you is that it will produce the hole you need.

The drill is just the required tool. You're not necessarily thinking about the hole: you're focusing on the painting you want to hang up or the books and photographs that you want to put onto the shelf.

So, as sales professionals, we have to turn our presentation upside down. Instead of talking about what we sell and what it does, we need to focus on why what it does matters to people. That is where so many salespeople struggle. If you only see the world from your side of the desk, your presentations will always explain to prospects what it is and what it does. Instead, all they want to know is:

"What's in it for me? How does this help ME?"

The solution?

You've got to describe the *sizzle* and not the *steak*.

You've got to talk about the *hole* they want to create rather than the *drill* they're going to need.

You've got to concentrate on the *itch* and not the *scratch*.

Do You Treat the Disease or the Patient?

"You treat a disease – you win/you lose.
You treat a person – I'll guarantee you'll win."

Robin Williams, in *Patch Adams*

Let's take the quote above, from the movie *Patch Adams*, and break it down into the two stages – treating the disease and treating the person – so that we can help our customers to recognise why it would be beneficial to work with us.

Treating the Disease

Imagine that you sold kettles and drove into a town where the concept of the modern kettle had not yet been introduced, completely unheard of. When turning up at each door, you said:

"I have a kettle; if you buy one, it will help you to boil water."

The majority of responses would most likely sound something like:

"I can already boil water, thank you. I have a pan and a stove."

You would find yourself selling to a town high on apathy and low on need.

Trying to discuss what it is (feature) and what it does (boils water) wouldn't get you through many doors. However, if your aim when knocking on the door was to try to help them and improve their situation, you would do so by attempting to explain what it does for them and why they should take an interest (benefit).

Treating the Person

Working this out properly needs a little thought. Put aside ten minutes at some point today, get yourself a pad of paper and a pen, and then write down the name of your product or service at the top of the page. When you've done that, answer these questions.

- Does this save people time, effort or embarrassment?
- Will they make more money if they take your advice or will this stop them from spending more money than they need to?
- Will this prevent some level of conflict or problem that they can happily live without?
- Will this make their life easier somehow?
- Will this give them the peace of mind they're looking for?
- What positive effects will becoming one of your customers have on them and the people whose opinion they care about?

Harnessing the Expert in the Room

How do you like to be treated when you need to purchase something but you're not an expert in that sector? What would you describe as a perfect experience?

After some windy weather one winter, I found myself having to mend some fence panels – and let me tell you, timber yards are way out of my comfort zone.

However, I'm glad to say (overjoyed actually) that there wasn't a single moment during my visit to that alpha-male enclave of wood when they made me feel foolish, uncomfortable, confused, patronised or, even worse, mocked because of my clear lack of knowledge.

Although any of those things could have happened, I just felt like I was being helped with a problem to which I desperately needed a solution – and, throughout the entire process, the discussion centred round what I was trying to achieve, i.e. getting my fence fixed.

So, here is my question: **would you say that your customers feel the same way when you're the expert in the room?**

If you can imagine how it feels to sit in your prospect's chair, and then learn to empathise with how they view your industry and the problems they face, you'll start suggesting solutions instead of products and creating conversations instead of delivering pitches.

Do the 180-degree turn and take a look at the world through your prospect's eyes. This simple exercise will enable you to have the conversations that they want to have with you – the kind of discussions where you try to help people and then they ask to buy things from you without the need for any sales trickery whatsoever.

DAMS: Overcoming the Four Types of Customer Objections

Contrary to popular belief, prospects aren't sitting in darkened rooms, trying to invent new, more fiendish objections for you to supply answers to.

Objections are just a fact of life in sales, but many sales professionals admit to having an irrational fear of them. In reality, the most common reason for salespeople disliking objections is the simple fact that they are not prepared for them. So how about we put them into four neat boxes and get ready to overcome each and every one? That would be useful, wouldn't it?

On the whole, objections are just another way for a prospect to say, "*I need more information*," and in many cases they indicate that the sale is not too far away. After all, if the objection is handled effectively, what reasons are left for the customer not to buy?

Even if someone has a real need for your product or service and you've kept that positive sale line running straight – neatly across the bottom of the chart, by building up and maintaining all that trust right from the beginning – there is a real chance that a great big "commitment gap" (see Chapter 1) will start to appear as soon as your customer begins to doubt whether this buying decision is really as great as you're making it out to be.

There are some sales gurus who will tell you that if you can deliver enough value during your questioning strategy and subsequent presentation, this stage can be happily missed out. Really?

You've been a customer too so you know how you react when you can feel that the salesperson appears to be winning you over too easily – almost everybody puts up some kind of barrier towards the end of a business transaction, even if it's just to make sure that they don't look like a complete pushover to everyone else involved.

In order to make that part of the sale as painless as possible, I like to break customers' objections down into four easy-to-remember groups, which I've shortened into the acronym DAMS: those seemingly unscalable barriers that block the natural course of a conversation and prevent it from flowing towards the final agreement.

DAMS stands for:
- **D**rawbacks
- **A**pathy
- **M**isunderstandings
- **S**cepticism.

Let's have a look at all of them, one by one.
- **Drawbacks**. Essentially, this refers to something you can't deliver, so understand it and get over it: you can't do it, the product doesn't do it or your company doesn't (or won't) do it. For example, if the customer wants a purple car but you don't make purple cars or when they want a house with a south-facing garden and all your gardens face north. Every salesperson has drawbacks in their portfolio and - despite all your concerns - your

competition won't have the perfect solution to every customer problem either. The answer is to outweigh the importance of the drawback with the heavier tonnage of all the benefits that your product or service can deliver. If all the good things that your product does fail to bring the scales crashing down towards a close then this probably isn't your prospect – or, worse, you haven't fully grasped how you really help your current clients.

- **Apathy**. This comes across when a customer shows little interest in your wares and can't see any good reason to move forward. Apathy is a tough one to crack because you're dealing with someone who sees no need for what you have to offer. The only way round apathy is to use your well-honed questioning and listening skills to help them uncover – by themselves – a previously unrealised need. You may have spotted an opportunity, but it's up to them to recognise the need. Once you've helped them to discover one or two items that they didn't even know they required, there's more than a fair chance that they will have moved beyond their apathy and onto considering the possibilities of what life would be like with these new options.

- **Misunderstandings**. If a customer suddenly makes a statement that's totally inaccurate, you've probably got a misunderstanding nestling in there somewhere.
A misunderstanding needs to be handled gently; if the customer has got the wrong end of the stick about something, they won't appreciate you highlighting it. If it's just the two of you, they'll feel stupid, whereas if there are others present, they'll be mortified. Neither of

those emotional states is going to make them feel happy about signing a contract.

- **Scepticism**. This final objection essentially boils down to your prospect doubting that your product or service will deliver all the wonderful things you say it will.
  When this happens, you need to introduce a little proof. You know the kind of thing: customer testimonials, brand presenters, some recent industry data, a demonstration, a test sample or some relevant magazine articles.

Good news, though: there's a silver bullet that can neutralise each objection. They all have a weak point and – with the right information and viewpoint - you'll discover that with all DAMS, there's always some way of getting over or going round.

Dealing with Drawbacks

A drawback usually crops up when your product or service is missing something that the customer believes is important to them.

The best way to think of this objection is by imagining a set of scales, where the most important weights are also the heaviest. So if importance equals weight, all we have to do is find a way of outweighing the drawback.

If you fill the other side of the scales with everything that your product or service has to offer and the scales don't budge, then they're not your customer.

However, if the other side of the scales is filled with features and benefits that are of interest to the customer, then the scales might eventually tip with their collective weight, and that's when the customer will decide that the conversation should continue.

You achieve this by:
- reminding the customer of the features, advantages and benefits that they have already shown an interest in
- continuing to ask the appropriate questions until you have uncovered enough importance to outweigh the drawback.

When it comes to appropriate questions, try using closed questions to summarise each item that the customer felt most positively about. This will also give you a chance to double-check that you haven't misjudged their position.

If what you have on your side of the scales still isn't heavy enough, you will need to introduce other important features, advantages and benefits by asking OVER questions (see Chapter 3) until you have uncovered the needs behind the opportunity and you can present a weighty enough case.

In order to handle a drawback, you need to have the entire picture in view and bring everything together with a phrase such as:

"Let's take a look at your total requirements and make sure we've got as many of them covered as possible."

Dealing with Apathy

Apathy is a particularly difficult attitude to handle, since an apathetic customer can't see any need for change or movement. More often than not, people tend to be apathetic because they:

- don't think they need what you're selling
- are happy with the service provider or product that they're currently using.

The strategy for turning apathy into interest is very similar to the one you would use when confronted by a drawback.

Apathy weighs heavy on the scales too, but this time it's much more stubborn.

You've got to ask the appropriate CUES (see Chapter 3) and OVER questions until you really know how you can help.

By the way, always try to make sure that you're picking the battles you can win. Of course, passionately try to help those who will clearly benefit from working with you, but if someone really doesn't need what you've got, that's not apathy: it's just a waste of your precious time.

In order to make sure that you know which instance you are dealing with, ask yourself these questions:

"Is this a genuine opportunity?"

"Will their situation be improved if they become my customer?"

*"What questions do I need to ask, so that I'll really
understand the extent to which I can help?"*

*"What questions could I ask that will enable the customer
to see how much I could help?"*

You will find that you only have to uncover one or two
hidden needs, in order to diminish their apathy; if you can
really help and they've recognised the problem, they should
be interested enough to continue.

Dealing with Misunderstandings

The first thing to recognise here is: misunderstandings are
never the prospect's fault; they are always down to the
salesperson.

It doesn't matter whether you have explained yourself a
thousand times or drawn pictures that a four-year-old would
understand. Telling them that *"they're clearly not bright
enough to recognise a simple concept when it's right in
front of their nose"* isn't going to win you the deal.

But here's the thing:

Nobody likes to be told they've got an ugly baby.

Belittling me or making me feel stupid – even if I'm the
only one in the room who feels as if you did – will lose you
the deal. Also, if I don't understand something that you
have come into my office to explain to me, how can it be
my fault? Surely, you can't have explained it well enough.

So, even if it is the fiftieth attempt, swallow your pride, hide your annoyance and say something along the lines of: *"Oh, I'm sorry. I haven't explained myself properly; actually, what I meant to say was…"*

With misunderstandings there is only one course of action to secure a positive outcome and that is:

You take the blame and you re-explain.

Dealing with Scepticism

When a customer expresses scepticism, you need to introduce some element of proof. Commonly used items include brochures, specification sheets, data from research studies, a live demonstration, magazine articles, professional journals, testimonial letters and third-party references.

You need to acquaint yourself with the proof sources for each of your products or services and you should know which ones are best for all the different scepticism-based objections you encounter (there are probably only about five that regularly reoccur).

You need to be prepared to offer the best examples of proof for every item that you sell, with the creative ability to tailor them to each individual prospect.

When you introduce your proof, make sure you avoid coming across as though you agree with the customer's scepticism, train yourself to use words which acknowledge their point of view but allow you to move onto your new solution without making it sound like a disagreement.

My favourite way of injecting a little proof into the conversation is with Zig Ziglar's "FEEL, FELT, FOUND" method. It works like this: *"I understand why you **FEEL** that way. [Insert the name of a previous happy customer here] **FELT** that way too – but what they **FOUND** was... [Insert the appropriate example here]."*

You End up Getting What You Settle for

In his book *The Secrets of Closing the Sale*, Zig Ziglar points out that:

"A sale is made on every presentation. The prospect either sells you that they can't or won't buy, or you sell them that they can and should buy."

Generally, this comes down to how you hear the conversation that you're having with your prospect.

Let me tell you another story…

An army of frogs (for that is how you refer to a bunch of frogs) were making their way through the woods when two of them fell down a deep hole.

When the other frogs saw how far down they'd fallen, they advised them to give up – they were as good as dead. But for some reason, those two frogs completely ignored this "helpful" advice and tried to jump out. While they were trying, the others kept shouting: *"Throw in the towel! Lie down peacefully and die!"*

Eventually, one of the unfortunate frogs recognised his situation, gave up, collapsed and died. But to everyone's surprise, the other one just kept on jumping with all his might, putting in even more effort than before. Once again, the frogs shouted down, *"Stop torturing yourself! Just accept it and die."*

After what seemed like forever, and with a mighty leap none had ever seen before or even thought possible, he made it out. As he pulled himself up, the other frogs asked, *"Didn't you hear what we were telling you?"*

"No," he said, *"I've had mud in my ears – I couldn't hear a word you were saying. I thought you were shouting encouragement!"*

So what do you hear when prospects bring up their objections?

Is it: *"I'm not convinced – I need more proof"*? Or perhaps it is: *"Are you joking? Who would want that?"*

How you feel about yourself and the thing that you're selling will make an enormous difference to the way you hear a prospect's concerns and objections, and unless they have no money – genuinely, no way of paying for it – then what you've got is either a perfect fit for them or not.

Unfortunately, you won't recognise objections as opportunities with mud in your ears – or a badly developed misconception of why you're actually there. There's no point getting upset with a prospect who can't see how perfect your solution is, and you're not helping anyone if you can't get that fact across professionally and effectively.

It's at that point that the prospect sells you that they can't or won't buy, or you sell them that they can and should buy.

**And let me tell you, you'll always
end up getting what you settle for**

"Repeat after me: 'Your price is too high.' 'Your price is too high.' 'Your price is too high.'"

5 | EXECUTE THE SOLUTION

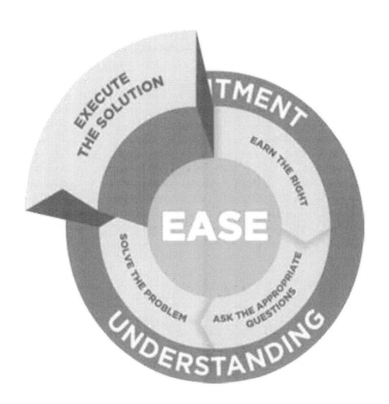

Gaining Customer Commitment and Delivering on Your Promises

As we move into the final quadrant of the sales cycle, we find ourselves back in the top half of the diagram, underneath the word COMMITMENT.

Once the customer understands how you can "Solve the problem", you will need to agree on a course of action that effectively gains their commitment to move forward, so that you can "Execute the solution". Amongst other things, this will involve: asking for the business, negotiating the best possible terms, filling in the required paperwork and staying true to your word.

The Two Scary Monsters Waiting for You Round the Corner

During training workshops, the two *"fears"* that I have noticed plague sales professionals the most are those of negotiation and closing.

Before we get into this section any deeper, I would like to point out that I'm not a big fan of what much of the sales world refers to as *closing*.

There are two distinct pictures that are painted in the mind when certain sales gurus describe the action of closing a sale. They either make it sound like you're trying to win some form of epic battle with your customer – where you need to find a way to break their spirit and then make off with their treasures – or they describe a number of hypnotic techniques that charm customers, in the same way that insects are attracted to a Venus flytrap.

Personally, I much prefer the description used by Neil Rackham in his book *SPIN Selling*:

> *"A close is anything which puts a customer in a position which involves some kind of commitment."*

Replacing the word *closing* with the words *gaining commitment* makes much more sense to me. I also think that referring to the tiny piece of the sales process where you ask for the business as *closing* gives it a false sense of

166 / Selling with EASE

finality – as if there's no more work to be done: we can just close everything and go home.

Of course, though, framing it as such fills some people with that ridiculously false hope that there might be one particular moment – a golden minute – when all the magic happens. Unfortunately, this promise always turns out to be just another bottle of snake oil, corked and labelled by those who make a living from pedalling short cuts and one-liners (useless and in many cases even morally questionable) to the desperate and lazy.

You need to have already proved that you are committed to help, gained your customer's trust right at the beginning and successfully moved through both of the "Understanding" quadrants (asking the appropriate questions and solving the problem). If you have ignored all these steps then there is nothing you can say that will help you to jump up the board onto the square labelled *"Use your close now and win the game"* during a genuine business transaction.

It's much more useful to understand that you're more likely to lead your sales conversation to a successful outcome if you:
1. summarise the problem
2. outline your solution
3. tell them how much that solution will cost
4. justify that cost
5. gain their commitment towards its successful execution.

When to Ask for the Sale

The main thing to remember here is that you are having a conversation with another human being because you have something to sell. It may sound obvious but it's surprising how many people get unnaturally shy and jittery towards the end of a business transaction.

Also, bear in mind that very few customers are polite enough, or have enough spare time to waste, to let you get this far if they're not really that interested. So the customer is well aware that you have something to sell and they are expecting you to ask for the business sooner or later – it's actually a bigger surprise when you don't.

They have no intention of begging you to sell them something, so it's up to you to muster the confidence and move things along. I have known some salespeople who were so desperate to avoid asking for the business that they talked themselves right past a sale. They just kept on with their pointless light banter and polite conversation for so long that they completely missed the moment, and the potential customer got bored and ended the appointment having bought absolutely nothing.

There are some salespeople who leave those meetings thinking that everything's gone brilliantly: everyone got on exceptionally well and they didn't offend anyone with any unnecessary sales talk. What they don't see, of course, is the competition walking in afterwards, taking the conversation to its natural conclusion and walking away with the contract.

Sometimes a customer can be likened to someone who loves to dance; sitting expectantly at the side of the ballroom, waiting to be invited onto the dancefloor but, although you might make eye contact, etiquette requires that they should always be the one who is asked to dance – never the other way round.

So, if you have had the good fortune of being invited to the ball but don't have the guts to walk up and ask them to dance when you have the opportunity, then you can't get upset when they eventually end up dancing with someone else.

I can understand that some salespeople might get a little nervous when reaching the point where they have to ask for the business; on occasions, it can be the first time during the conversation where the buyer has the opportunity to introduce a little negativity or even plainly say no. But if you don't take the risk of getting one or two No's, then you're going to miss out on an awful lot of YES's.

From the moment a salesperson meets a buyer, everything which is said or done is part of – and leading up to – this point. In truth, there's nothing wrong with closing as early as you can. That doesn't mean rushing through the first three parts of the sales process; it just means that once you have noticed that the customer wishes to move forward, you help them to do so – and you ask for the next dance.

Let the Customer Do the Closing

Which of these situations do you think is more likely to lead to a successful sale?

- You ask the customer if they would like to buy something.
- The customer asks you when they can have it.

That's right: it's far easier to make a sale when the customer is enquiring about how to make the purchase.

By the way, it might surprise you to know that customers do this all the time – i.e. ask if they can buy something – but salespeople can become extremely hard of hearing every time it happens. It's almost as if they don't want to believe it can be that easy.

There's no art to this: you don't have to develop a special sixth sense or be in touch with any particular cosmic vibrations. When the time is right, the customer will let you know that they are ready to move forward. They trust you, you've listened and understood them, and you've shown them how you can help – why shouldn't they ask what they have to do next? It's the next logical step.

Unfortunately, many salespeople either miss the signs completely or trample over a timid little buying signal like a herd of rampaging wildebeest.

In order to get this right, you have to be listening out for certain words and phrases that your customer will use – and then, rather strangely, you have to gain their commitment by asking an open question.

And it's this open question that makes all the difference.

Closing With an Open Question

Think about how you would react if your customer said something like: *"How soon can I have it?"*

Many salespeople would respond by giving them the date and/or time (e.g. *"You can have it on Friday before midday."*). That would seem obvious, wouldn't it? I mean, the customer asks when they can have it, so you give them the answer.

But that's actually how you can trample over your chance of gaining commitment and walk straight past your sale.

Let's take a look at a couple of likely scenarios.

Customer: *"How soon can I have it?"*
Salesperson: *"I can have it with you by Friday."*
Customer: *"Oh, that's not bad."*

Where does that take us to? It takes us to the salesperson still having to ask for the sale, that's where. And as we recognised previously, that's our second choice; what we want instead is for the customer to do the closing.

Let's start from the same point and try again.

Customer: *"How soon can I have it?"*
Salesperson: *"Is there a date you need to have it by?"*
Customer: *"Ideally, before next week."*

And there it is: so subtle that most people would miss it.

- The customer asks a question.
- The salesperson then asks an open question to gain some form of commitment and a little more detail.
- The customer responds positively, with a suitable time frame.

This allows the conversation to move onto something like this...

Salesperson: *"Would you like me to check if we can get it to you by Friday?"*
Customer: *"Yes, please."*
Salesperson: *"What would be the best time for delivery?"*
Customer: *"Sometime in the morning."*

So what happened there?

- The salesperson asked a closed question to clarify understanding.
- The customer responded positively.
- The salesperson asked another open question to gain further commitment.
- The customer responded positively with a more exact time frame.

If a customer shows some level of interest and the salesperson immediately jumps on the opportunity (usually due to a huge sense of relief and a little bit of quiet desperation), they run the risk of creating another commitment gap, which can cause problems at this late stage of the game.

Remember: *if you tell me what I need to know to be able to easily say no, I'll probably say no.*

However, if you take your time and ask questions that positively encourage the customer to make small commitments – questions that allow them to tell you what they want, when they want it and how much of it they'll need – then you're pretty much just helping the customer to write out their own order form.

Also, try to make sure you don't trample all over your customer's more subtle buying signals with your uncontainable excitement. I have watched far too many salespeople completely ignore, talk over or walk right past phrases like: *"Go on then, I'll give it a try!"* The same rules apply: make sure you ask a great question.

In fact, test yourself now. If one of your customers said: *"Yes, please, I'd like to place an order,"* which open questions could you use to make sure that you've squeezed every ounce of commitment out of the opportunity?

Different Types of Closes

Whenever anyone mentions closing techniques, I picture sleazy salespeople from yesteryear, con men who trick old ladies into giving up their life savings and street hustlers who hoodwink unsuspecting tourists.

However, presenting all of these techniques like that here would be completely disingenuous of me, because I use some of them all the time. Not in a sneaky, trying-to-be-clever kind of way, though. I introduce them into conversations because they're really good at sucking the ambiguity out of a sales call.

So try to look past the cheesy names that these perfectly respectable sales tools have been landed with and work out which ones can help you to release the confirmation and commitment needed to bring your next sales conversation to a natural close.

Assumptive

If you can get to grips with comfortably delivering the assumptive close, you'll pretty much find asking for the business (and every other kind of close) a cinch.

Essentially, you make the assumption that everything is going ahead and so you ask for the business – well, why wouldn't you? Here is an example:

"OK, are you happy with everything and ready to move forward?"

Alternative

This one is really useful and great for closing just about anything from appointment dates to customer commitment. Once both you and the customer have decided to move forward, you offer two or three alternatives so that you get confirmation of what's required and when. Here are a couple of examples:

"Do you want to order 12 bottles or 24?"

"Would you like to book the appointment on Tuesday or Thursday?"

This is actually an extension of the assumptive close, as you are assuming that the requirement for an order or appointment has already been agreed.

Future Benefit

Use this one when it would be beneficial for the customer to order now rather than waiting, such as before an imminent price rise or tax increase. Here is an example:

"Rather than wait, would you like to make sure the order is invoiced and delivered before the budget increases come into play next month?"

Elimination

This is when you ask a question to make sure that there is nothing left that could get in the way of signing the deal and that you have dealt with any possible reason for not moving forward. Here is an example:

"Is there any reason you can think of why we shouldn't go ahead?"

This close is best used when you're fairly sure that you've handled all possible objections. Otherwise, it's not a close at all but simply another understanding question (which takes you back to quadrants two and three – "Ask the appropriate questions" and "Solve the problem").

Bracket

This one is quite useful if you're writing multi-layered proposals or when you're dealing with a customer who has indicated that one option won't be enough.

You lay out three choices or three different possibilities for moving forward.

- Offer 1: luxurious, expensive and at the very edge of where you believe their current budget lies; however, not so out of reach that they wouldn't consider it at all. You want it to be something that they would really like and aspire to – hey, if they go for it, happy days!
- Offer 2: the deal you expect to be the one they'll take.
- Offer 3: the bargain-basement deal.

Apart from giving you a chance to ensure that you're not aiming too low and losing out on a more substantial piece of business, you're also helping the customer to put their purchase into perspective. By rejecting the top-end option, they can feel good about not breaking the bank, while discarding Offer 3 allows them to feel that they have invested in a certain level of quality.

An Abridged Encyclopaedia of Closing

There are many closes that I haven't mentioned here, but if you want to go looking, you will find them in the many sales courses and books (and free web pages) devoted to learning them all in detail – if that's what you really think you need. However, I'm going to stick to my principles here so I've only written about the ones that I believe work naturally when you've managed to get the selling bit right and that belong within the entire "Selling with EASE" process and philosophy.

Why? Well, mostly because, in this day and age, the average customer knows exactly when they're being *sold at* and they definitely recognise that cold feeling of unease creeping up their spine when someone is trying to manipulate them.

Although I chose not to list them here, there are closes that work perfectly well and even some that you can use to convince wavering customers to move forward today rather than walk away and forget about you tomorrow.

For example, you could use the Ben Franklin Close: you draw two columns on a piece of paper to describe, on one side, all the reasons why they should buy from you and on the other (shorter) side the reasons why they shouldn't. Or how about the Calculator Close? You start working on your calculator, saying things like: *"Less discount"* and *"Minus new customer adjustment"*, and then show your incredible deal to the excited, expectant customer.

And let's not forget the Golden Bridge Close, based on a strategy put forward by Sun Tzu, the Chinese general who wrote *The Art of War*. One piece of advice in this book is to: *"Build your enemies a golden bridge"* – in other words, guide them towards the precise direction in which you want them to go and then, instead of cornering them and forcing them to fight you to the death, give them a little space and allow them to leave with dignity. The Golden Bridge Close works in a similar way: you close off all other possible options except the path you want your customer to go down.

I could go on mentioning many, many more but these closes aren't about helping people to make great buying decisions; they're short cuts for lazy salespeople trying to find some easy form of manipulation, so that they don't have to bother showing customers what a difference they could make. It's just another attempt to try a little sleight of hand and weasel the sale out from the customer any way they can.

But what they don't realise is this: most of those salespeople will try to close in exactly the same way as a child attempting to perform a card trick without the appropriate amount of practice. In both cases, the cheesy patter is embarrassingly unnatural, the delivery is fumbled and uncomfortable, and absolutely everyone watching can see the "*magic*" coming from a mile away.

Undoubtedly, just as the kid's parents clap supportively anyway, some of those poor customers might need what's being sold so much that they'll overlook their discomfort to get it. However, the sad outcome of both scenarios is the same: on hearing the applause, some children will think they've got the whole magician thing nailed and will never feel the need to improve or practise to perfect their technique. In the same way, most of those salespeople will think it was their Jedi Mind Trick close that got the deal and, holding on to this belief, will convince themselves that their overall sales performance completely rocked.

Purchasing 101

Do you know why most of your customers ask you for a discount?

It's because almost every salesperson they have ever asked previously got a little flustered and then knocked the price down without the tiniest struggle or complaint (although sometimes they might of had to ask their boss first).

On top of that, there's also a pride and social standing thing going on. I mean, imagine going for a drink with your friends just after you've bought a second-hand car and someone asks: *"So that new car of yours, how much discount did you get? What did you offer them?"*

And you say, *"I didn't ask for a discount. I thought the advertised price was quite reasonable."*

Surely all your friends would look at you aghast and exclaim, *"You did what?"*

This is the point when you either explain why it's great value or get really upset, as you start to agree with them and realise that you might have been ripped off. That belief – however strong or weak – will be solely based on the conversation you had and the explanations you received from the salesperson.

So here's another scenario: let's say that you swapped a bag of three magic beans (your product) with a customer for their family cow (their money). Afterwards, if they went to meet their friends for a drink and proudly showed off your three magic beans, would they come chasing after you and demand their cow back? Or has your customer received such an amazing sales experience that they will start to explain how miraculous the beans really are and why they were worth every single penny?

It's Definitely Not All about Price

I recently spent some time with a group of extremely senior salespeople from one of the world's largest companies, who insisted that all their customers' buying decisions were down to price.

No, they're not.

Take, for example, their business. Those ten senior salespeople, their big cars and expense accounts – not to mention all the support staff who make things happen for them behind the scenes – would easily represent a cost per salesperson of around $150,000 a year.

Therefore, that team of ten cost at least $1,500,000 to keep on the road – and they were a tiny percentage of the entire sales force. So I suggested to them that if all their problems were indeed down to price – and the sales team could make no difference whatsoever – then surely getting rid of just those ten salespeople and changing the business model to a click-down menu on a website would save the business in excess of a million dollars. In fact, if we did that, we could knock a dollar off a million units immediately – if it was all down to price then that's the problem solved.

No sales team required: everyone buys on price and now it's affordable.

That particular sales team didn't like that idea very much at all. But that, unfortunately, is the undeniable truth. If the sales team don't know or can't explain the difference between their business and a lesser priced competitor, they become an expensive folly.

Of course a professional buyer is going to hammer everyone down on price; that's their job. But that doesn't mean to say they want to end up with cheap tat or something that won't get the job done.

The advice I'm going to give you is the same I gave to that team: work out the five most potent reasons why you are better value than the competition and then learn how to explain that to your customers.

Remember: evangelists don't try to tell you about Heaven to secure their place – they're already going. They tell you because they don't want you to miss out on Paradise. They would consider it a sin if they didn't share the opportunity with you.

That is how you should be with your product or service. Get in there and help prospects to make great buying decisions before some con artist tries to rip them off, overcharge them, or sell them something they don't need or even want.

How Much Does a Tennis Ball Cost?

When I was about eight years old, there was a sign in the corner shop window for tennis balls. Suddenly filled with an overwhelming urge to buy one, I rushed home and asked my mother if I could have the money. To my surprise, she said: *"Yes, OK. How much do you need?"*

Flushed with a strange sense of embarrassment which I still can't fully explain, mixed with some kind of self-destructive paranoia, I knocked the price down by about 30%.

I still don't know why I did that; maybe I only like delivering good news, maybe I didn't think she'd give me the full amount or maybe I thought it sounded better – in any case, I got less than I actually needed, making the whole process a little pointless.

When I got back to the store, the only thing I could afford was a ping pong ball, which I bought (to ensure the trip hadn't been a complete waste of time) and then hid it from my mother because I felt completely stupid.

I'm telling you this because this memory came rushing (embarrassingly) back to me last week when I overheard a business negotiation and the salesperson reacted in a nearly identical way, which got me thinking: *"How many grown-*

ups are doing something similar with their company's money?"

Price objections really embarrass some people. Sometimes, when a salesperson has been given some flexibility with the final price point to help them *"get the business"*, there's a nervous inner voice that desperately wants to knock a little off. It whispers that the amount being asked is quite possibly a little on the high side and, anyway, the margin flexibility that the company has given them was probably built in for a moment just like this.

The trouble is, that little voice starts chatting even before the customer asks for a discount.

Let me tell you another story...

Skip ahead about fourteen years from the tennis ball debacle and I'm working for a business that imports the most expensive, stylish and technologically cutting edge aquariums around at the time. If you wanted one of those, you took your home aquarium hobby *really* seriously.

So, one day this guy calls and asks if we have a certain model in stock; I check the storeroom and call him back to tell him that it's available for collection that day and will cost $1,000, all wired up and ready to go.

So the chap arrives in his large European hatchback, parks up right outside the double doors of the industrial unit and opens the trunk of the car in preparation. As he walks into the showroom, the most senior salesman in the business pushes past everyone, introduces himself and gives a brief demonstration of the ready and waiting aquarium. After all this, the customer asks: *"How much discount for cash?"*

Mr Senior Salesman replies, *"10%"*

So the customer pulls out $1,000 in cash from his wallet, counts $100 from the top and gives the senior salesman $900.

I was young, new and inexperienced, but I was also a bit shocked. The business hadn't made me aware of any 10% discount rule; of course, I knew that there was a bit of flexibility to get a deal if we asked, but I was fairly sure that there was nothing in the induction about 10% cash discounts.

The senior salesman walked past me, waved the $900 dollars in the air, winked at me and said: *"And that, my boy, is how you make a sale."*

So, let's have a look at that again...

The customer had clearly come equipped to buy the aquarium; he had called to check its price, travelled to pick it up, prepared his car to take it home and brought the full amount in cash.

So why did the salesman feel the need to give him a discount?

Maybe, like the eight-year-old me, he only liked delivering good news, maybe he didn't think he'd get the full amount or maybe he thought it sounded better. In any case, he got less than he actually could have obtained – 10% less to be exact.

Could you imagine increasing your turnover by 10%? It's a lot harder than decreasing it by 10%, that's for sure.

Are you ever embarrassed when you tell people how much they will have to pay for your product or service? If so, why is that? If you are ripping them off then, quite rightly, you should feel ashamed; get out while you can and find a product which you can feel proud of.

But if it's worth it, if the price is fair, what's your problem?

Here's another way to look at the *"It's all about price"* statement: were those shoes you wear to work the very cheapest on the high street?

I bet they weren't. I'll bet someone out there was selling cheaper shoes than you bought that day; so why did you spend more than you had to? Was it because you liked the colour and the style? Did they make you feel good about yourself? Was it because they were a really nice fit? Or maybe they were just practical and did exactly what you were looking for.

How to React to a Price Objection

As we've already discussed, everybody gets price objections and everyone gets asked for a discount at one time or another. However, there are a few really easy pieces of advice to follow, which might just save your business a fortune.

Agree, Argue or Apologise

The first thing I want you to do is... nothing – nothing at all. Be absolutely quiet. Don't say a word. You see, you've got to make sure that your customer has actually finished talking. What if they were just taking a breath or gathering their thoughts?

When a customer raises any kind of price objection, the three negative options available to you are:

* agree
* argue
* apologise.

If you agree, you're confirming that you're about to rip them off with something that isn't worth the money.

If you start arguing, your customer will most likely mirror your response or just get up and leave.

And what exactly are you apologising for?

188 / Selling with EASE

Nevertheless, when customers say something like *"That's expensive..."*, the salesperson often jumps in with one of those three responses. And what do you think that does to the trust generated or the chances of their business relationship continuing with any level of genuine equality? How does the customer feel after the salesperson reacts with any of those three responses?

As an example, my local dry cleaning company was taken over recently by new owners and when I went to pick up my suit, I noticed that all the prices had gone up. So I mentioned this to the lady behind the counter and expressed my surprise at how much it now cost to get all my suits dry cleaned. Her reply was: *"Sorry, I know. I wouldn't come here if I needed anything cleaning. It's a complete rip-off!"*

She managed to apologise and agree with a price concern all in the same sentence – that's someone who definitely isn't looking after their long-term job security.

So what should you do?

Well, the next time your customer says something like: *"That's expensive..."*, don't just move on to Plan B and throw a bit of a discount into the mix.

Instead, wait and see if they finish off with something like: *"That's expensive... But I guess you get what you pay for"* or *"That's expensive... But I did promise my kids I'd get one before the summer."*

How Surprised Are You When You Get a Price Objection?

Are you surprised when someone tells you that you're too expensive? No? Well, you should be.

The expression on your face should read, *"What do you mean? It's a fair price! I don't understand."* And – on top of that – you should mean it. Don't act surprised; be surprised.

If you walked into an Aston Martin dealership and told the salesperson that the car you were looking at was overpriced, they would look slightly taken aback and then reply with something along the lines of: *"No, it's not overpriced. That's just how much an Aston Martin costs."*

So, do you feel *that* proud about your own products or services? Do you have the necessary belief in the quality of the things you sell so that you'll stand your ground when people accidently mix up cost for value?

What if They Still Think You're too Expensive?

If your expression alone hasn't moved the conversation forward and, even though you kept quiet, they've said all they're going to say on the subject, then it's time to ask a question because, quite frankly, no one has a satisfactory answer to the statement: *"It's too expensive."*

However, you can formulate an appropriate response if you ask something like:
- *"In what way?"*

- *"How do you mean?"*
- *"What makes you say that?"*
- *"Compared to what?"*

Don't react or make assumptions; instead, clarify why they're saying the things they're saying and thinking what they're thinking.

This may take you back to quadrant three – "Solve the problem" – and to understanding and overcoming a DAMS objection that you hadn't previously uncovered or laid to rest. But don't worry; it just means you missed something in your rush to get here – no biggie.

A Couple of Things You Should Know about Discounts

Nobody puts in less effort after giving a discount.

Who in your organisation is going to do less, if you needlessly give away some money?

- Will the production team wrap things up using cheaper packaging?
- Will the delivery team use less fuel or ask to be paid for fewer hours?
- Will marketing give back some of their budget?
- Will IT need fewer computers?

The answer to all these questions is: no, of course they won't.

What we sell is either worth what we're charging or it's not. Instead of letting your customer tell you why it's not, confidently charge full price and make sure you can justify the value.

Our childhood memories guide most of our discounting decisions.

While growing up, any person who could give a discount or had the ability to *"knock a bit off"* appeared to our young and impressionable eyes as an incredibly important individual.

They would stand proudly next to the item for sale and, with a cheesy smile, say something like: *"Yes, the price is indeed $500 but since you're nice people (and thanks to my incredible benevolence), I'm going to knock that down to $480!"*

These people were giving away money – how important do you have to be to be able to do that?

Now that you're a grown-up, you probably realise that this perception wasn't exactly accurate. You are able to recognise that the people who give you discounts aren't titans of industry or leaders of business.

Millionaires and billionaires aren't rich because they feel the need to give away money to make them feel important. On the contrary: they're wealthy because they *don't* give away their money. Having the power to discount might make you feel influential, but it won't earn you any respect (or friendship) from your customers – and it certainly won't make you rich and powerful.

Here's the truth about introducing discount generosity into a business situation:

"You'll never bank thanks once you've started to breed greed."

In other words, if you start out trying to help people (which is all we've talked about so far throughout this book) then you'll find that they expect (and are quite willing) to pay the going rate for that help in all commercial environments.

However, if you begin to give that help away – even one tiny slice at a time – then all you do is diminish its value.

That wonderful moment at the end of the sale that is normally filled with gratitude from a happy customer will almost certainly become engulfed in greed. Instead of feeling joy at receiving the perfect solution, your customer will start to wonder how much further they can push you.

Full pipelines don't need to give discounts.

If you have too many customers waiting to buy what you sell, you'll never give anything away. Just think about the brands, companies and businesses that don't need to offer you discounts. That five-star restaurant, luxury car manufacturer, famous wedding dress designer… What do they all have in common? Full order books – and it's not by accident.

Fill your pipeline – business coming out of your ears – and the notion of people asking for a discount will sound hilarious because you're already at capacity.

Simple.

Sometimes it's not a discount; it's a concession.

In a customer's mind, a discount means that you must have been overcharging them. But that's not the same as making a concession for something like:
- early payment
- buying in bulk
- preferential status
- testimonials or references.

By giving a discount, all you do is justify what everyone already thinks about salespeople. However, if they wish to improve your trading terms then what subsequently becomes available might be an adjustment due to renewed circumstances.

You see, that's a completely different deal.

When we're selling fruit, each fruit has its own price. If someone wants to buy an apple, the price of the apple never changes. But if someone wants to order all our apples, or pay a certain sum before the harvest, then we might have to factor in renewed costs with regard to logistics or the possible advantage of a guaranteed bank balance.

What's the Difference Between Selling and Negotiating?

If your job involves some element of business-to-business sales interaction, it may also involve some level of negotiation.

Many salespeople aren't natural negotiators, which is not necessarily a bad thing or a lost cause. It's just that the personality traits demonstrated by great B2B salespeople and commercial account managers usually have more to do with being helpful than being hard-nosed. But that's why a lot of account managers stumble and struggle to differentiate between the two: selling and negotiating.

Continuing – or having to restart – selling during a negotiation may very well be seen as a sign of weakness (or fear) and it's definitely a sign that you didn't use your precious selling time well enough when you had the chance.

On the other hand, if you dive in and start to negotiate before you've finished selling then the customer won't have any real chance to recognise the true value of what you have to offer.

There are a number of sales negotiation courses which tend to have more in common with Special Forces training camps than business development workshops – and they rarely help those who really need it. Although they're a great couple of days out for those thrusty, gung-ho, do-or-die members of the sales team (everybody knows at least one), they are far less helpful for Bob, who just wants to know how to ensure that he gets an aisle-end display for Christmas, or Susan, who has got her third phase of price increases to push through.

You see, there are quite a few glaring differences between the skills required to be an exceptional influencer, business partner and brand ambassador, and those required to become a top-notch negotiator.

For instance...
- Selling is about matching a problem with a solution and showing someone how you can help – that's not negotiating.
- Selling also involves explaining and presenting the total value of your product or service and the benefit to the customer of moving forward with you, rather than going with someone else – that's also not negotiating.

Negotiating can only happen after all the selling has been completed, once both sides are ready to move forward and seek a mutually satisfactory agreement. It is all about two parties trying to get the best deal available for their own side of the table and this discussion definitely shouldn't be mistaken for a price objection; if you've started negotiating then any objections should have already been overcome.

Moreover, negotiation has certainly nothing to do with winning – your customers aren't the competition; that's the... erm... competition (you know, the other people who want the same business you're negotiating for).

Negotiating may also involve an element of bartering, wrangling, haggling, hard bargaining, dealing, concession trading and defending your position – and that is definitely not selling.

Here's another way to think about it: when you've finished selling, you're probably going to put in your proposal. On how many occasions this year – after submitting your proposal – have you INCREASED THE PRICE because the customer requested further negotiations?

So, before you begin to negotiate, ensure that you've finished selling, which means being certain that you've packed in every piece of value you could muster. Otherwise, you'll just end up building your sales castle on a foundation of sand. And a castle built on sand is never a good place to defend anything.

Beware the Stare and Be Prepared

Don't you hate it when you're sent to negotiate with a buyer who clearly has the upper hand? As you park your car and walk towards reception, you can almost hear the entire purchasing department chanting softly: *"You need our business more than we need you – sharpen your pencil or make way for a supplier who will!"*

And of course, back at base, your boss has no sympathy – no sympathy at all.

But it doesn't have to be that way.

Here are four pieces of advice to ensure that future negotiations will be a little more even-handed.

Stop Trying to Win

Let's tackle the big one first.

In the past, every time you walked into a negotiation intent on winning, your emotions took charge of your brain.

Put simply: if you enter a negotiation trying to win then all I have to do is make you THINK you've won to get what I want.

As an alternative, why not enter every negotiation with the intention of securing the best deal for you and your business.

Handy negotiation tip #1: during your next negotiation help your customer to "win", while you concentrate on securing the best possible outcome.

It's Time to Believe in Your Solution

What you believe to be the truth and how you feel about it create a silent message that you send across the table throughout negotiations.

John Wyndham's sci-fi novel *The Midwich Cuckoos* (which was turned into the 1960 film *Village of the Damned*, with the tag line: "Beware the stare that will paralyse the will of the world!") involves alien children with spooky powers. One of those unearthly powers was the ability to read minds. In order to fight against this threat, all the human adults imagined an impregnable wall shielding their thoughts, but the children were too strong and their mental barriers tumbled.

Similarly, your poker face might very well be a Las Vegas fortune waiting to happen, but I'm afraid it won't work when you're sitting in a business negotiation, worried that they're reading your mind and you're thinking: *"They know I'm bluffing. The competition have offered them something for peanuts – I'm going to have to offer them the knock-down price my boss said I should keep up my sleeve."*

Handy negotiation tip #2: become evangelical about what you sell, and its true value and worth.

Essentially, I'd like you to think of it like this: when the customer breaks down your defensive mental wall and appears to be reading your mind, you should be thinking: *"I can't believe you don't want this – are you mad? There is nothing that will do the job better."*

Don't Start Negotiating Until You've Finished Selling

Some people think that negotiating is just another stage in the sales process but, as I pointed out previously, that actually might prove to be your undoing.

If you have to re-explain the value to your customer during a negotiation then you never finished the sales process. It will be seen, at best, as an indicator that you and your company are not quite up to the job – or as a sign of nerves – and at worst as open season for ripping your proposal to pieces and offering to pay you three beans for your bag of diamonds.

Handy negotiation tip #3: explain and present the total value of your offering, and why moving forward with you is the best option available to them, during the sales process. Only negotiate once this process is over.

If they need what you've got and you're their best choice, you're in a much stronger position than you think – which brings me onto…

Focus on Their Worries and Try to Forget about Yours

What thoughts do you believe occupy a buyer's mind during a negotiation? What emotions do you think they feel as they organise their pencils on the meeting room table before you arrive?

In the same way that you're sent in with the responsibility of bringing home the bacon for your business, those buyers are tasked with making the best buying decisions by their hierarchy.

So, what happens if they get that wrong?

Well, apart from the commercial and financial implications, there's the chance of a little personal humiliation and – in certain cases – the risk of losing their job.

But what happens if they make the buying decision of the year?

Yup: promotion, a fat bonus, heaps of praise – good times.

So what do you want your customers to feel before they pick up the negotiation stick again?
- Anxiety: "If I choose this one, people will think I'm an idiot."
- Apathy: "I can live without this – maybe I'll take a couple if they're giving them away."
- Excitement: "When I present this internally, people are going to think I'm a purchasing genius."

Handy negotiation tip #4: during a negotiation, what you know about the buyer's situation will guide every decision you make – but so does what you don't know.

Ask great questions throughout the sales process so that you thoroughly understand the problem you're solving and can point out why your option is the only one worth taking, before those negotiation tactics and tricks start to fly across the table at you.

The Negotiation Secrets of Professional Buyers

They're a sneaky group of people, those professional buyers.

First of all, they have the audacity to go and get more training and external advice than 90% of their opposite numbers in sales ever do. Then they have the intelligence and foresight to remember the course material and content, and use it appropriately.

Is there no end to their devilry?

If you feel that you or your team have been hit with the "*buyer stick*" once too often, have a quick look through the list below and accept the fact that – to quote Felix Dennis – it's:

"A silly game, with serious rules".

It's up to you, however, to decide whether that game involves a scary cat and a sales mouse or two professional businesspeople working towards a mutually agreeable conclusion.

So let's avoid being hit with that buyer stick any more than we have to be; put on your hard hat and start to recognise when the following "tactics" are being aimed at you.

- **Good buyers know their goals and targets**. They know what they want to achieve – the little bits and bobs, as well as the big stuff. There's a fair chance that they've prepared properly and given this a lot more thought than you have. They have a firm grasp of what they want and what they need, and a deep understanding of the difference between the two.

- **They are trying to figure out your weaknesses**. Some will act ethically, whereas others won't, but if they spot something that they can use, you can bet your bottom dollar that they'll file it away and bring it up at just the right time.

- **They use the "*wince*" to their advantage**. When they want you to know that they don't like the way things are heading, they use the "*wince*". When deployed properly, it's followed by a cold silence to send out a clear, unambiguous signal – and the ball is squarely back in your court.

- **They are more than happy to use silence without feeling any level of discomfort**. Salespeople hate dead air, so buyers add lots of space when they comment and respond. If you feel the need to pointlessly fill the void with your own voice, they will gain the upper hand. And why are they are so comfortable with silence? Simple: it only took a couple of instances to prove that its use would pay them back time and time again – now they know it can't fail.

- **They have anticipated your position**. They roughly know what you want to achieve and need to walk away with. They then watch for clues as you are presenting, keeping their eyes and ears open. They've also learnt to filter out their own subjective viewpoint and, during this period, focus on you – you are not the only one asking open questions, or hadn't you noticed?

- **They deserve an OSCAR® for the use of emotional bombshells**. It might be anger, over-the-top agitation or even tears. But before you start passing the Kleenex or cowering under the desk, remember that they are trying to achieve something, and if they manage to emotionally pull you away from your focus then you will no longer be aiming straight. They, on the other hand, are well aware of what they're trying to achieve and their focus will be completely intact.

- **They decided on the bottom line long before you turned up**. They know what they are OK with leaving on the table, and they know what they have to take with them when they walk out the door.

- **They have smokescreens and anti-ballistic devices ready and waiting for you**. They will try to distract and deflect you away from getting too close to the bottom line, and use minor details to derail you from the points you want addressed.

So What's the Answer?

A funny thing happens in the minds of many sales managers when they think their team might lack the required negotiation skills. For some reason they decide to send them all on courses that are better suited to people who have to bargain the release of war zone hostages or to keep them up until midnight for a week, like a group of trainee Navy Seals on their final initiation test.

First of all, in a training or learning environment people tend not to take in very much useful information when they're completely exhausted. Secondly, if your team have got to a point where they're simply *"negotiating"* how much of your margin they're giving away, with absolutely nothing left in their bag to trade with, then:

- it wasn't their inability to storm an embassy held by terrorists that was in question – it was the fact that, during the first half of the sale process, they couldn't effectively explain and help the customer to understand the true VALUE of your proposal
- it certainly didn't depend on how they coped with sleep deprivation, while solving puzzles and being bullied by a short, angry man with a military haircut.

Right at the beginning of the sales process:

- you plan. You're not just ready for the ride – you pack for the entire trip
- you understand the true value of your proposition
- you believe in that value and present it fanatically
- you are prepared to overcome all reasonable objections – including pricing
- you know when you have to walk away.

A client said something to me recently, with regard to relationships, that I think works really well in this context:

"Everybody will break your heart one day. You've just got to work out which ones are worth it."

© 2003 Ted Goff

"Did I leave my umbrella here last week when I was telling you about our new high-quality machine parts that will save you a lot of money?"

6 | PLANNING, PREPARATION AND POST-CALL PROMISES

210 / Selling with EASE

Make Every Customer Call
Effective and Meaningful

There can often be some confusion and a variety of different answers when you ask a group of salespeople to define what qualifies as a truly effective sales call. You wouldn't think it would be that hard to clarify, but actually one of the main issues I come across (and something that sales directors often ask me to help them correct) is that when salespeople meet or call new prospects on the telephone, they appear to completely forget their purpose for being there. These are a few examples of phrases I hear from business-to-business sales teams on a fairly regular basis:

"I just call in to show my face."

"I want them to get to know me before they get to know what I'm selling."

"I don't want to upset things by revealing I'm actually there to sell them something too soon."

"I'm investing promotional support early in the hope that one day they'll become a customer."

"When you call a prospect, the quickest way to get them to hang up is admit that you're selling something."

My first – and best – bit of advice to those salespeople is: you should always know why you're calling (what you're trying to achieve) and fully understand how you can help (and how you've helped previous customers) long before you even pick up the phone or knock on the door.

When you make a genuine sales call on a prospect or customer – whether face to face or on the phone – your objectives will probably fall into one of three categories:

- prospective
- improvement
- remedial.

In other words, if it really is a genuine sales call, you'll be trying to:

- find out whether you can become a supplier (prospective)
- develop an existing customer into something more (improvement)
- put something right that's recently gone wrong so that you can carry on trading (remedial).

Calling with a Purpose

If you pick up the telephone to book an appointment with me, then book that appointment; if you come over to my restaurant to sell me wine, then sell me some wine; if something has gone wrong, come in with an excellent plan to put it right – whatever the reason for interrupting my busy day, it should be the one and only thing you intend to talk to me about.

Prospects and customers are never sitting by the phone or staring at their computer with nothing else to do, wishing a salesperson would call to save them from their loneliness.

The reality is: we're all busy.

If you call me then I'll probably want you off the phone or out of the building as quickly as possible. Why? Because I have a whole list of things planned to do that day – and you almost certainly aren't on that list.

I'm not being rude; I just need to remain focused because I've got so many plates spinning and can't afford to let a single one drop. It doesn't mean that I definitely don't need to talk to you, but if I do, then you've got to make sure that you stick to the subject so I can get straight back to what I was doing before you distracted me.

Set Yourself "Best" and "Tolerable" Outcomes

Let's say that you now know exactly what you want to get out of your next sales call. You know precisely why you're making the call, what you want to talk about and what you want to achieve, so you set yourself a target.

So what happens if you don't achieve the target you've set for that call? Is that it? Are there only two outcomes? Is it simply a choice between win or lose, death or glory?

Those appear to be the odds that most salespeople give themselves – they walk in, thinking: *This will either go well or it won't; they will either buy this or they won't.*

What if that didn't have to be the case? What if we could find a third way, something that would enable us to achieve a positive outcome every time we made contact with a genuine prospect or customer?

Well, I've got the answer to help you discover just how to do that.

Have a think about the next sales call you're going to make to a prospect or customer. Now work out what your **BEST** intended outcome could be for that call – what's the greatest thing that could happen?

Don't think small here – thinking small is something we're going to save for a little later in the process. For now I want you to dream *really* big.

There's a great quote from Og Mandino's small but powerful book *The Greatest Salesman in the World* that perfectly sums up the way I want you to think:

> *"Is it not better to aim your spear at the moon and strike only an eagle than to aim your spear at the eagle, and strike only a rock?"*

So what's the very best thing that could happen? Make sure this decision stretches you past your comfort zone. If it doesn't scare you a little, it's not far enough. Now think hard about what it is you want to achieve during your next sales call. Got it? Good, write it down somewhere so you can't change your mind. What you have just decided upon is what I like to call your "best intended outcome" (BIO).

I have a quick message for all of you who are now looking at your crazy, unreachable target and thinking: *"This is ridiculous. There's no point in even trying because it's never going to happen."* This isn't about being optimistic or pessimistic; it is about being realistic and practical. If that is the best thing that could possibly happen then that is where we should aim our sights – why wouldn't we?

Liberating a caged exotic bird from captivity only for you to then keep it in a box would be an odd thing to do, wouldn't it? Wild birds are meant to fly, so let it fly – what is there to be afraid of?

I know that's a strange analogy, but that's pretty much the same as uncovering an incredible business opportunity and then not taking advantage of it, simply because you think it might not come to fruition. Why hide away a perfectly good business opportunity? What's there to be afraid of?

You could also look at this from another angle: if you decide that the chances of hitting the moon are low, then you'll probably set your target lower, which might be fine for you, but what about the customer? Have you ever thought that maybe they need to change, move on or find something new? Why not make the customer aware of all the options available and then let them choose for themselves?

Of course, we're still realists, so we know that the best thing that *could* happen *might not* happen every time. So what we need is some form of gradient that takes us all the way down to what will become our "tolerable intended outcome" (TIO).

This ladder of options will allow us to test the water throughout the call, checking which opportunities are available to us at the time.

Let's look at an example: if you worked for a window cleaning company and a prospect (who owns the largest office building in the city) agreed to see you for a meeting, then you might set your best intended outcome as a three-year contract to clean every window once a week.

Unfortunately, during the call you discover that they're happy with their current window cleaners; they arranged the meeting just to find out who you are and what you do.

So you take a couple of steps down from your best intended outcome and ask if they would agree to giving you the contract for one floor of windows – as a test – for a month so you can prove how reliable, professional and effective you are.

Sadly, they don't want that to happen either. So you take a couple more steps down through your possible outcomes and ask them when the next chance to bid for the full contract will be. They reply that they're not sure and advise you to send in a proposal so they'll get in touch when they're ready. The trouble with this situation is that it would take you past a tolerable outcome - as you would have no control over what would happen next.

So how do you set yourself the lowest rung of the positive outcome ladder? The only rule you need to remember is that it can be as far removed from your best intended outcome as you like, but it has to be something that involves you – and that *something* has to make a difference and continue to move the process positively forward somehow, even if it's only a tiny step in the right direction.

A tolerable intended outcome can't leave the customer in charge of calling you, or with you agreeing to put a brochure or proposal in the post. You must be clear about what happens next and be in control of that action.

What people seem to forget is that you can't control the actions of anyone else; the only person you can control is yourself. So your tolerable intended outcome needs to involve something like:

- agreeing the date and time for a follow-up telephone call – that *you* will make

- putting the next meeting in both diaries
- organising a demonstration.

Whatever it is, it has to be an action that *you* will be taking.

The great thing about creating both a TIO and BIO is that if you don't hit a home run on your first attempt, you're in control of when you're going to get a chance to bat again. On top of that, as your prospects will now be expecting what's going to happen next, you will always have a diary teeming with opportunities.

Superb Meeting, Perfect Proposal… So Why Won't They Take Your Call?

So you've had your meeting, planned your call, set your objectives and achieved every single one of them – how could anything go wrong? By the way, the meeting was *AMAZING*. They immediately agreed that everything you recommended was perfect for them; every time you uncovered a need and matched it to a feature, they swooned. Whenever you expanded those features to the corresponding advantages and benefits, their eyes smiled and they had to stop themselves from clapping like four-year-olds on the best Christmas morning ever. Your proposal – *my goodness your proposal* – dripped with passion and flair; it put forward the case for change like nothing you had ever written before.

Back at the office, you walk like the sales star that you are – you haven't actually told anyone it's in the bag but your boss has seen the twinkle in your eye and knows that something special is coming your way.

SO – WHY – WON'T – THEY – TAKE – YOUR – CALL?

What's happened to their manic enthusiasm for moving forward?

"I'm sorry, there doesn't seem to be anyone around!" is the pre-programmed response from everyone who picks up the phone – even when you're trying to be clever with different extensions. It just doesn't make sense.

As with most things in sales, salvaging what has gone wrong is rarely impossible, but learning how to avoid getting yourself in that position in the first place is a much better place to start.

Let me take you back to that meeting… You've done all the wonderful things mentioned above and then your client says: *"So what do we do now?"*

You: *"Well, I'll put a proposal together, get it over to you and then I'll give you a call to move things forward."*
Prospect: *"Fabulous! Talk to you in a couple of weeks."*
You: *"Wonderful! Thanks for your time – great to meet you."*

Salesperson exits stage left, while the prospect appears to have gone onto a witness relocation programme and is never heard from again.

The big problem here is… There wasn't actually an agreed level of commitment from the prospect – just an assumption of one.

In a business-to-business sales situation – especially the big stuff – you'll rarely get a signature or full agreement before a proposal and then the proposal always needs to be followed up. But while the salesperson is walking out, clicking their heels, the sale has already gone cold.

Let's run that meeting again.

Prospect: *"So what do we do now?"*
You: *"Well, I'll put a proposal together and get it over to you this week."*
Prospect: *"That sounds great."*
You: *"Wonderful! I really want to make sure this moves forward the way you want it to so, with that in mind, I'm back in the area on the 15th and 19th – which one would be best to have our follow-up meeting?"*

And there it is: the thing that's so obvious once it's made obvious. Organising the next meeting before the proposal reaches them ensures that you get to talk to them about it once it's written, close the sale and put it to bed.

And if they won't book a follow-up meeting? Then, unfortunately, the meeting probably didn't go quite as well as you thought.

How Do You View Opportunity?

There is an old sales story that goes something like this...

In 1865 two shoe salesmen from rival companies were sent to a remote part of Africa for the very first time. Both were highly regarded for their ability and viewed as the best salesperson within their businesses.

After weeks of travelling, they discovered a group of indigenous people and it became immediately apparent that no one in the tribe – or any of the neighbouring tribes – wore shoes.

So both men hurried back to London to relay the news to their respective board members and employers. As soon as the ship landed, they raced to their offices and, throwing open the large wooden doors to the boardroom, the first one announced:

"Stop! Scrap the plans to build another factory! There's no business to be had there; nobody wears shoes!"

On the other hand, the second chap burst into his offices and shouted:

"Quick! We need to build a factory over there; nobody wears shoes yet!"

So, when you walk in to see a prospect who doesn't currently buy whatever it is you sell, what does your belief system tell you? What does the little voice say at the back of your brain?

Do you believe that you are looking at someone who has made a decision never to wear shoes or do you see, instead, someone who just hasn't been shown the right footwear yet?

Don't chase impossible rainbows, but be aware of your opportunities, make sure you are ready for them to surface and then grab them with both hands.

However, if you have a feeling deep down that every time you call on a customer you're just being a nuisance or interrupting their day unnecessarily, then you:

- haven't worked out how you really help existing customers
- don't have faith in your company, product or service
- might have ended up in the wrong job.

Making Sure Your Opportunities Match Your Targets

Sometimes it can be really easy to mix up genuine sales meetings with promotional, marketing or service calls. When required, the latter can be incredibly useful but they tend to have completely different objectives to those that will eventually grow our business and help us to hit our targets.

So here's a quick way to work out whether the calls you make on a day-to-day basis are actually matching up with the objectives that your company has set. If you're making a genuine sales call (prospective or improvement) and it goes well, the customer will tell you *"I need that"* or *"I want that"*, or ask *"How soon can we get started?"*

If you're making a service call (remedial) or a promotional call and it goes well, the customer will give you a *"Thank you"* – and mean it. And if you listen carefully, you'll find that the word which customers use with the most feeling during a pointless coffee call is: *"Goodbye"*.

So ask yourself – before you make your next customer call – which one of the following would you most like to achieve?

- An order
- A thank you
- A goodbye

224 / Selling with EASE

If your wages are based on increasing or maintaining business then your employer is probably hoping for an order but, hey, if everything goes well and you're brilliant at what you do, you will probably end up with all three. On the other hand, if the main aim of your role is as an ambassador for the business – delivering some level of customer service, marketing or promotional support – then they'd probably be happy with a heartfelt thank you and a pleasant goodbye.

However, if the most positive description that you can give for the majority of your calls is that people quite like your company and don't mind you being there, then there's a fair chance that sales meetings and appraisals aren't your favourite times of the year.

If you haven't given any of this much thought before – and I have to say, at the beginning of my career I certainly hadn't – then you probably need to take a step back and have a think about why someone pays you that much money to drive around and drink coffee with strangers.

Every time you walk through the front door of a business, you are there:
- as a customer
- as a professional with an idea, product or service that can help
- just to get in the way.

Before you go in to see your next customer, work out which one of those you'd most like to be viewed as.

How Do You Mentally Prepare for a Sales Call?

I was once asked during a sales training session for my views on the best way for a salesperson to set themselves up mentally before going to see a client. So I told them about Andy, a great sales manager I had at the beginning of my career.

During my induction, and while I was learning the ropes under his watchful eye, we had to drive to a prospective customer's office, so I made sure that I had some of his favourite music in the car – cassettes in those days – to keep him entertained during the journey, but also in an effort to ensure he wouldn't ask any of those pesky questions that sales managers so love to ask on the way to a call.

Andy just turned the music off and started to talk calmly about the prospect we were going to see – and that's when I got my first lesson in sales preparation.

Why Are You Nervous?

Worry and panic come from lack of preparation – you're frightened of the things you're not ready for (and that includes questions, objections and achieving your desired outcomes) – so you have to make sure that you've looked up your prospect on the most informative online platform at your disposal, checked out their business website and also have some idea of who their current suppliers are.

Why Aren't You Nervous?

Being prepared and ready for anything is fine; however, being overconfident and cocky is just plain foolish. There will always be a small chance that something could take you unaware, however long in the tooth and experienced you might be. The day you get too comfortable and start to take your customers for granted is the day when those young, hungry sales wolves sneak up behind you and snatch the food off your plate.

Why Do They Want to See You?

Why is this busy buyer willing to give up their time to see a salesperson? It's certainly not because they're lonely. Take a few minutes to work this out and then write the reason in big letters in the middle of a blank sheet of paper. Surround it with questions that they might ask you and that you might ask them, together with a few solutions which will explain how you might help them solve their problem.

On top of that...

- Triple-check that you've got everything you need before you set off – you are bound to forget something, so stop and work out what it might be before you climb in your car.
- Have an agenda (even if you only use it to take notes or to jot down all the points you want to bring up).

- Bring to mind how you, your product, service and company have helped others in a similar situation; have examples of those happy customers ready and memorised.
- Go in to help – not because it's your job, but because you definitely can and genuinely want to.
- You are a professional coming in to see if you can be of assistance. If some prospects don't want to accept your help (and some won't) then that has got to be their loss. Exude that belief – without mixing in even a hint of arrogance – and you will be amazed at how many people will treat you with the respect you deserve.

After that, make sure that you walk in with your head held high and your shirt tucked in – and then you just get in there and do your best.

Is Your Sales Pipeline Boiling Over?

There is a wise old saying that tells us: "*A watched kettle never boils.*"

I reckon if you watch a plugged-in, switched-on kettle long enough and it doesn't boil, your appliance is probably broken. Of course the phrase originated before electricity, but it was still nonsense back then. If your kettle wasn't boiling, your fire clearly wasn't burning hot enough or the kettle was too far away from the heat – watching it made no difference. I know, I know – I'm just being facetious; the saying is simply a way of pointing out that physically waiting for something or watching it happen won't bring it on any quicker.

But if you've ever found yourself staring at your computer screen, hitting the "send/receive" button and hoping that a few surprise enquiries will just drop in out of the blue to get things bubbling, then you probably already know where I'm heading with this analogy.

Here are a few pieces of modern "*sales wisdom*" doing the rounds – you may have heard a few recently yourself.

"*There's no business out there.*"

"*Nobody's buying.*"

"These days, you just can't get through to the decision maker."

"Customers never return our calls."

"No one is attracting prospects like they used to."

"It's not about value; it's all down to price."

"It's the wrong time of year."

If you hear these lines – or spout any of them yourself – take two minutes to answer these next three questions.

- It's never the content of the kettle that's at fault, if a fire is required, then you have to light one; so, what is it that you *really* need to do to get started?
- Once you've organised the initial flame, you'll want to get things on the boil as quickly as possible; so how will you get as close as you can to the heat without burning your fingers?
- What can you do next to stoke the fire so that it burns even more fiercely?

I challenge you to answer these with solutions that you can implement immediately and without blaming the marketing department even once.

"Our website has gone live!
That phone should start ringing
with orders any minute now."

7 | THE REAL SECRETS OF SALES SUCCESS

What Type of Salesperson Are You?

In my experience, all salespeople fall into one of three categories:
- can't afford to lose them
- can't afford to keep them
- can't afford to leave.

Can't Afford to Lose Them

Certain individuals deliver so much value that it usually takes half their working life for the pay structure to catch up with their actual worth – not just because of the business and profit they bring in for the organisation, but also the safe pair of hands and broad shoulders they possess.

They tend to be walking that extra mile before anyone even has the chance to ask.

When it comes to pay, giving them a few additional percentage points once a year is a drop in the ocean compared to what they're worth. That's why good managers constantly try to warn them about the fragility of value; the world turns, new ways turn into yesterday's fads, and modern techniques can become embarrassing and old-fashioned.

If you find yourself in this category, please remember this:

Trees don't grow all the way to the sun – everything stops somewhere.

Individuals need to constantly evolve – your current perceived value is just that: what you're perceived to be worth today. When that value becomes the norm across the team, you will suddenly become the oldest, highest-paid member of your peer group.

Sadly, you will feel neither old nor highly paid. And that is why you must continually find ways to become better tomorrow than you were yesterday; don't rest on your laurels or past successes.

Unfortunately, there are those who think that their current star can never dim and, very shortly after that point, they drop into one of the following two groups.

Can't Afford to Keep Them

I originally named this category *"Can't Afford to Pay Them"* but I thought that might insinuate that we couldn't afford to keep them because they were too good – but that's rarely the case. As I mentioned previously, money is always available for incredible talent.

The trouble is, when there ceases to be enough value, it just becomes bad business.

This group divides into a further two camps:
- the amount of profit they bring in doesn't cover their overall cost (wages, expenses, car, pension, tax, etc.)

- the amount of internal company distraction they cause means that you can end up paying three people to do one person's job.

Let me tell you a quick story.

I once put together a new business development team for a children's charity.

The team I inherited were taking more out in wages than they were bringing in from commercial donors – in fact, there would have been more money in the kitty for sick children if their roles hadn't existed at all.

When I pointed this out, one of them stood up and said: *"You don't understand; we're doing this for the kids!"*

My response was that they might have been doing it for their own kids, but at that time, the children the charity was created and designed to help were receiving no benefit whatsoever from the existence of that team.

Now, everyone would agree that depleting a pot of money from a children's charity and disguising it as an unproductive wage is morally wrong. But most members of the "Can't afford to keep them" group believe that it's perfectly reasonable to do the same thing in a commercial environment without feeling a single pang of guilt.

Can't Afford to Leave

You know who you are.

Your pay packet has continued to grow year after successful year and you thought that just being you, mixed with all that experience, was going to cut it forever.

Nope!

Hey, don't worry! We're not going to get rid of you straight away. You do an alright job. But we're not going to promote you either and, sooner or later, those recently promoted whizz-kids are going to catch you up – and they'll cost a bag of cash less than you do.

So, before you start to feel trapped, bitter and bored, IMPROVE YOURSELF! Try to become more valuable.

In fact, become so valuable that the competition start taking an interest in you at trade events and your own business decides that you belong firmly back in the "Can't afford to lose them" category.

It's up to you. You don't have to end up stuck in the same position, with the same company, until you eventually end up on next year's redundancy list.

But if you're going for interviews and they feel you're already over-priced then you probably are. I distinctly remember one particular morning, when a chap walked in for a senior sales job interview with a swagger from a 1930s detective movie, sat across the boardroom table and told the company directors why he was *so* the real deal.

After a great 45 minutes, we were impressed and he asked: *"So, how much does the position pay?"*

It's a fair question and, as we're happy to do what it takes to get the best, we replied: *"Don't worry; we'll pay you what you're worth."*

So he exclaimed: *"But I'm already earning more than that!"*

The "Can't Afford to Leave" brigade spends all its time trying to find someone who is willing to pay a premium price for standard goods. The trouble with that kind of thinking is that, as soon as the buyer discovers their mistake, they often require a refund.

Remember: people don't mind paying; they just don't want to overpay. So when it comes to looking for that next position, don't waste your time trying to polish the scratches out of the dependable old company car that's never let anyone down but has seen better days. Instead, give yourself an upgrade and find out how to offer them a Ferrari.

The Real Secret to Sales Success

There's a secret to business success which, if you're already putting it into practice on a regular basis – that's probably only around 5% of all the salespeople out there, so I think it's worth sharing – won't be that much of a big surprise.

It took me quite a long time to recognise this little nugget of truth for what it really is and then distil it into just a couple of short, memorable sentences – but here they are.

The reason why my career soared, while others around me splashed around in a muddy pool of bitterness and mediocrity, was down to this simple fact:

I went out and found new opportunities for my employers – most people want their employers to show them where the opportunities can be found.

Go on, read it again; it's deeper than you think.

Most businesses seek to hire salespeople who can uncover previously undiscovered opportunities, increase their market share and deliver value in the form of new business and profit. However, once employed, most salespeople (despite all the passion and confidence exhibited during the recruitment stages) will very quickly start to blame the lack of new business being generated on their brand, their marketing department or their competition.

They were hoping for warm leads so that they could just drive over to pick up the paperwork and then take all the glory (and commission) for "*the sale*".

That's not discovering; that's being shown – and it's not selling; it's order-taking.

So don't wait to be given business by your employers and then expect to be thanked for driving over to collect it; go out and *get* business.

That's how my career stepped up – one rung at a time – and kept on rising: when there didn't appear to be any business, I found a way to create the opportunity. When there was a shortage of customers, I went out and found some prospects.

When the fishermen went home hungry and defeated, telling me not to bother even trying, the first thing I did was dredge the pond in case there was something in there that they'd missed. Then I hiked over to the next lake and tried again, while they all went to the pub and talked about the one that got away.

Hey, sometimes I went home with less than they did.

But they made a habit of giving up, whereas I made a habit of never giving in.

Some will tell you that the secret of success is simply rising and then staying above mediocrity – and that's not far wrong. I'll add to that and say that while you're pulling yourself above mediocrity, make sure you also develop your tenacity and positivity muscles.

I'm not better than anyone else – or smarter or more knowledgeable – and I've never been given a better patch with better prospects than my colleagues. It's just that when people gave me the opportunity (and wage) to go and grow their business, I didn't expect them to give me leads on a plate.

I went out and found business for them – and brought it back with my tail wagging.

So the real secret is this:

> *Below-average salespeople wait for their business to create sales leads. Above-average salespeople create business opportunities and become Sales Leaders.*

(Average performers, who aren't putting in the effort, are just riding a wave of luck, which never lasts long.)

You can sit at your desk, just hoping and hitting the send/receive button if you like. Alternatively, you could leave it to chance, waiting for social media campaigns, your website or the marketing department to bring prospects directly to your door – and, hey, it might happen. But that's the same business everyone around you has access to – including the competition. It was coming anyway, with or without a salesperson to pick it up.

There's a reason why diamonds are tough to uncover: the really valuable stuff isn't found just lying on the beach for anyone to pick up. Fill your pipeline with pebbles if you want, but diamonds are what they'll congratulate you for.

242 / Selling with EASE

So where should you start? Where's all this business
hiding?
- You find it with new clients.
- You find it with disgruntled old clients.
- You look for new opportunities within existing clients.
- You portfolio sell across the board.

On top of that...
- Don't moan when there's no business; it's your job to
  find it – go and get some.
- Don't treat customers like one-night stands; learn how
  you genuinely help and watch your results prosper
  when you start to put that into practice.
- Learn what you don't know and get better at the stuff
  you do.
- Listen to, emulate and take advice from winners –
  never whiners.
- Stop trying to find the quick way of doing absolutely
  everything – find the most effective way and then
  perfect it.

Then do one more call every day after what used to be your
last call; over 40 weeks a year this equals 200 extra calls. If
we work on one in ten, ask yourself: what would 20 more
opportunities do for your pipeline?

Passing the Internal Customer Test

Isn't it strange that certain colleagues – and in some cases entire departments – feel the need to make our jobs harder than they already are?

You might be able to bring to mind a number of contenders within your business, as you read this short story.

The Hot-air Balloon and the Salesperson

There once was a man travelling in a hot-air balloon who suddenly realised he was completely lost. As he lowered himself down through the clouds, he found himself over a small, pretty garden where a woman was tending to some roses.

"Excuse me!" shouted the man. *"Can you please tell me where I am?"*

"Why, of course!" replied the woman. *"You are just above my garden!"*

The man in the hot-air balloon looked incredibly cross, took a deep breath and asked, *"Are you in SALES, Madam?"*

Astonished, she responded, *"Why, yes! However did you know?"*

To which he replied, *"Well, I asked you for some help and now that you've given it to me I'm no better off than I was before I asked!"*

"Oh!" His attitude and lack of gratitude had taken the lady by surprise, so she asked, *"Are you in Marketing?"*

The smug expression drained from the man's face. *"I most certainly am! How on Earth did you deduce that?"*

"Simple, really," declared the lady. *"You appear to have set off with no real direction or back-up plan and when it all went wrong, you came down from on high in search of some help. In order to offer you that help, I stopped what I was doing and now that I have, your incompetence appears to have somehow become my fault!"*

This story has always amused me, mostly because of the way it mirrors the internal politics I often witness in so many of the companies I work with. Of course, it doesn't have to be sales and marketing – it could just as easily be finance and production or HR and logistics.

One of the best bits of advice I was ever given was relayed to me by an old boss, who explained how I should look after and nurture my relationships with colleagues from other internal departments: my internal customers.

He didn't tell me to go about it with a sleazy, false approach (e.g. *"I don't really like you, but here are some doughnuts, so now can you do me a favour?"*). His advice forced me to think more along the lines of: *"Everyone here deserves my respect for the job they do and I'd probably like them to respect me, too."*

I can almost guarantee that every time I deliver one of our customer service workshops and explain that their organisation's customer service philosophy needs to be adopted for internal customers just as much as external ones, someone in the room will say something along the lines of: *"You've got the wrong group in here – the xxxxxx department should be doing this, not us!"* Or even: *"The whole company should be attending this workshop! We'd be so much more efficient if everyone treated each other in this way."*

You might not think it's worth the effort – most people don't see the point without having the time and guidance to really think it through – but the knock-on effects of treating internal departments to the same standard of service and courtesy that the company expects front line staff to extend to external, paying customers can seriously improve your own success (as well as ensuring that all the other departments make your team's requirements a priority, which is an added bonus).

And to make this deal even sweeter, you really don't have to do anything particularly ground-breaking to become a star internally.

Have you any idea how all the other departments currently view your team?
Sorry to upset you, but it's probably not as positively as you think. So, time for that to change!

Just start by asking yourself this simple question:

After any interaction with you or your team, how do you want your internal customers to describe the experience to others?

Make a note of the keywords, emotions and actions that you'd like them to use when describing what it's like to have you as a colleague.

And there's your answer:

JUST DO THOSE THINGS FROM NOW!

If you and your team act in that way from now on, that's how people will talk about you and that's how they'll feel after dealing with you.

So, why should you care? Well, a clear conscience and an untarnished reputation are already two half-decent reasons. But how about: because nobody else in your organisation has ever stood back and thought about doing it? Actually, nobody else really has any idea why they should even try. By adopting this approach, you will end up working in – or running – the department with the best reputation in the entire business.

SUCCESS!

Learn to Sell Lemonade and You Can Sell Anything

One weekend last summer, my nine-year-old daughter decided to set up a lemonade stand at the front of the house as her first commercial enterprise. To be fair, she'd been nagging me to help her do it for over a year – ever since she saw a bank advert where a girl of a similar age did the same thing.

I only realise now that right up until the point when she set up her tiny table and chair (sandwiched between her hand-drawn poster and little plastic till), I was acting like your typical *"Don't go into business"* advisor. I recognise this because I heard so many similar voices before I set up my first company.

"Are you sure you want to do this? What happens if no one comes? You might end up looking silly. Is what you make really good enough for someone else's money?"

But, like all good entrepreneurs and pioneers, she was able to filter all that nonsense out and went ahead with what she knew to be right.

So, here are a few things that a nine-year-old girl selling home-made lemonade could teach some seasoned salespeople I've met along the way.

1. She sat down and worked out her USP (Unique Selling Proposition).
I didn't intend for it to sound like a mean-spirited question, but I also didn't want to see her little disappointed face at the end of the day, so I thought she should ready herself for success rather than just sitting out there and hoping for the best.

"So, why is anybody going to buy this, honey?"
"Why wouldn't they?"
"Well, there's a lot of competition. We don't live far from the local pub and a can of fizzy drink from the shop is only a dollar – why would they stop and buy yours?"

So she sat down, thought about it and then redesigned her poster to explain why people should buy from her – in fact, she had five reasons why her lemonade was worth stopping for.

Question: what are the five reasons why people buy your product or service instead of the competition's?

2. She knew why it was worth the money.
It would have been really easy to spend $15 on ingredients and plastic cups, and then just let her play shop – but I could tell she wanted to do this properly. Once we put all the costs down on paper, she realised what price we couldn't go below, and why, and we justified it with facts.

Question: when someone raises a price objection, do you get a slightly uneasy feeling, mixed with the inexplicable need to knock a little bit off, or can you justify the value and the cost to both yourself and your customers?

3. **She was ready for objections**.

We sat down together and I pretended to be an awkward customer. I gave her every reason I could think of why I wouldn't buy lemonade off the side of the road from a nine-year-old girl. We then came up with conversation pieces that overcame drawbacks, apathy, misunderstandings and scepticism – I don't think I've ever been so proud.

Question: what five objections do you regularly get? Have you sat down and worked out how to overcome each one so that they will no longer be a problem?

4. **She was passionate about the work**.

Two days she sat out there, at the front of the house. There was no stopping her, she wanted to do it and set up her stand straight after breakfast – in fact, we had trouble getting her back in the house for lunch and dinner.

She chatted, she poured, and she would disappear for a few moments and then return with complimentary bowls of water for the customers who had dogs. Admittedly, it seemed to come quite naturally to her, but she wasn't daunted by anything or anyone. Intelligently, she delegated most of the grunt work to me (concentrating instead on the actions that would bring in the most money) and what was plain for all to see was that she really, really enjoyed it.

Question: when was the last time you sprang out of bed and went looking for new customers? Can you honestly say that you spend all your time on actions that move you continuously closer to achieving your goals and targets?

Giving up Is Not an Option

When sales figures start to slip and slide in the wrong direction, the manner in which a sales team react and respond will have a huge impact on whether those results ever turn back around or not.

When sales calls become an endless cycle of potential customers who have no interest in hearing what you have to say, many salespeople just start to become quieter and less active; they forget the reason why they're picking up a wage and some even begin to apologise for wasting a prospect's time before they've started selling anything at all.

In my youth, I spent a bit of time singing and playing in bands, and we played some really rough gigs – and I mean *scary* rough. These were not the kind of audiences you dream about as a kid, where everyone, packed like sardines along the front of the stage, is clapping along, peering over the footlights and staring up through the dry ice at you.

When you play a working men's club on a Saturday night, the audience are all huddled round small four-man tables, most of them facing away from the stage and talking (loudly), while a few at the back play cards, pool or dominos.

There was always a line of wide-shouldered men, heavy with the scent of cheap aftershave, leaning against the back wall, sneering – willing you to be bad – waiting for that moment when they could turn back to the bar and complain about the quality of bands that were continuously booked by the useless club manager.

It's at that point that performers can either go on stage and become a self-fulfilling prophecy or decide to get up there and give the room one hell of a good night out. That's your choice as you wait in the wings, clutching your guitar or holding on to your drumsticks.

Prancing around on stage in front of a room oozing disinterest can make you feel really stupid but unless you reach out and try to engage, nothing's ever going to change. So when I didn't have their attention, I just sung louder.

I would focus on each group, try to make them turn round one by one, and increase the passion in my voice and the power of my delivery. I would hold notes until I was ready to pass out, while the lead guitarist would stand with one foot on the monitors at the front of the stage and play solos that made people lean forward in their chair with admiration. When our band played, people stopped what they were doing and turned round – and, whether you loved us or hated us, we put everything into giving you the best Saturday night out you'd had in ages.

You can see something similar happening in the television singing competition *The Voice*. During the blind auditions – when the coaches have their backs to the stage, only turning round if they like what they hear and want the singer to join their team – the contestants tend to fall into two distinct groups.

As the time ticks down, and the four coaches' chairs continue to face the audience, some of the singers just start to go through the motions; you can see in their eyes that they're thinking: *"Oh well, it wasn't meant to be. I did my best... Never mind!"*

But there's another group who aren't thinking like that at all. They start attacking the back of those chairs, like medieval knights laying siege to a castle. They catapult emotion after emotion over the top; they ram every ounce of passion into every single note. This group are thinking: *"I came here to sing for you tonight and you are going to hear me. I will pour everything I have into this and reach out to you. I will move you so much that you will feel this performance shake your very soul."*

Salespeople tend to fall into groups that are remarkably similar, so you have to decide. You can choose to join the sales gang that says, *"What's the point? We've got all the business we're going to get; it's just not worth the extra effort,"* or the much smaller group who never stop thinking: *"If you don't listen to me, you will be missing out. You'll love this! Give it a chance; I know it's just what you've been waiting for."*

The latter is the one that adapts to the situation at hand, never loses focus of the goal and continuously strives to improve.

The Best Three Lessons of My Sales Career

I have to be honest here. One of the main reasons I've been so successful in sales and sales management is simply because, throughout my career, a small group of believers saw my potential (which, through large parts of my early career, I managed to hide extremely well) and then had the tenacity and patience to help me see it too.

I've quite literally filled books with the lessons they passed on, but here are just three that made a huge difference.

Lesson #1: Deliver Value to the Business or Get out

When I was growing up, few people who knew us would have ever referred to my family as wealthy, and by the time I hit my teens, I had still never met anyone who I'd now classify as rich. Therefore, I aspired to very little other than to possibly one day own my own home and drive a car. If I could pay the rent and have enough cash left over to fill the fridge with good food and drink a few beers at the weekend with the boys, I was happy enough.

My first business-to-business sales role was a tough education, but they invested time and money into my development, and in return I put my suit on every day and polished my shoes. Just earning the flat basic wage didn't bother me at all. It would have been nice to receive a little bit more commission every month, but if it didn't happen, it wasn't the end of the world. I turned up for work with a smile and hoped that sales would follow me in – but if they didn't, hey, no worries.

I have to say, it came as quite a bit of a shock when they fired me.

And although I don't remember that particular sales manager as one of my favourite all-time bosses, he did me a huge favour.

That experience changed my outlook on sales forever. There was no way I was ever going to fall over so stupidly ever again. So in every role that followed I made sure that I was making a difference and that the people who mattered noticed it.

Lesson #2: Understand How You Can Help, but Be Different

For a good few years I walked in to see customers and sold *at* them. That's how everyone I knew presented their wares and, sadly, it's still how most people I meet sell to this very day.

Even after a week of solid, expensive and highly focused sales training with a big multinational company, I still had no concept of how I helped anyone. We didn't talk about it; we weren't trained on it – no one internally saw it as a requirement, or cared that it might be a better way of doing things or produce more business.

It was a buyer called Terry Wiseman who helped me to see it one Christmas. He worked for a regional wholesaler and told me, in no uncertain terms, that my generic "Christmas promotion" was completely pointless.

That year I sold five boxes through Terry's business.

The following Christmas I held up my hands, admitting that my ignorance towards customer buying motives and arrogant attitude weren't going to deliver either of us any bonus – and that's when he opened my eyes.

He showed me why people bought my products, how they used them and what they needed them for, as well as what flicked their switch, the quantity they liked to purchase and the add-on purchases that could be acquired with the right bundle deal.

That Christmas I sold 10,000 boxes through Terry's business.

This lesson was definitely worth its weight in gold; Terry helped me to see something that I would later describe like this:

People buy drills because they want to create holes – bad salespeople present drills; great salespeople help them to achieve the hole they need.

Lesson #3: Make Sure You Can Go Back Again

So now my career is going through the roof. Company-wide memos referencing my big wins are coming from the

Managing Director's office, I'm getting personal letters of thanks from the Chairman, and I'm regularly asked to host sales meetings to share my insight and techniques with the rest of the business. I've had two promotions in six months and I'm being considered for another – a big one – before Easter.

And that was when my Sales Director dropped a bombshell during my end-of-year appraisal. He looked up from the standard paperwork and said: "*I know what you're doing, Chris – and it's time to stop.*"

"*What do you mean 'what I'm doing'?*" the indestructible me replied. "*I'll tell you what I'm doing: I'm knocking every sales target out of the park, I'm securing contracts that were previously thought unwinnable on a monthly basis and I'm getting listings that no one has got anywhere near achieving in the last 20 years – that's what I'm doing!*"

The memory of his stare still fills me with a chill and leaves me feeling stupid, foolish and arrogant 20 years after the event. He put his pen on the appraisal document and, slowly and precisely, pointed out that my search for glory was about to fall flat on its own fat backside.

Yes, I had a knack for helping people, delivering the solution they needed and writing proposals that they actually wanted to read – and, yes, that had led to business going through the roof. But that was the last time a customer ever heard from me.

Even when things went wrong or didn't work out as well as I'd promised, I left their calls unanswered – I was too busy chasing the company-wide recognition, the next big win. But that industry – just like every other – was too small to treat existing customers so badly. My thinking was at least six months short of short-term thinking.

Contracts and tenders would come round again in a matter of months, and new product launches would require presentations to the same groups of people. Even if I moved to another business, appointments would be few and far between because I'd lost their trust – and testimonials and referrals were just about to dry up and never return.

He also pointed out that further down the line, when I had my own sales team to manage, their reputation would be tainted by mine and no one would want to see them either, so that would end in failure too.

I nodded in embarrassment; as his expression stretched into a smile, he told me that my future was bright so I should stop acting like a wounded baby bird and do something about getting it back on track – and then he went and bought me a drink to toast my continued success.

The Twenty-first-century Sales Gym

Salesman Bob has just renewed his "Sales Gym" membership for another year.

He's decided that he wants to get himself ready for the testing times ahead: healthy, wealthy and thinking like a champion. All the members of his Sales Gym know that if you want to have your membership considered for renewal, you have got to master the Century 21 Business Treadmill.

Bob's been around a while. He watches his unprepared peers climb onto the treadmill's black rubber tracks and press the start button. Some of them find that they can't keep up with its demanding pace and just stop running. However, if you stand still on a fast-moving Century 21 Business Treadmill, it will take your feet from underneath you and you go down – *hard*.

There's actually a big sign hanging above the Century 21 Business Treadmill that new members rarely ever read; it says: *"Get off, keep going or fall over"*.

If you manage to stay on and keep up, you can watch your progress steadily climb on the little monitor and those around you will comment on how well you're doing, which is quite pleasant.

Every now and then the incline will rise uncomfortably; you see, this model has a random *Recession Setting* – it very quickly gets steeper, slower and harder. During those times, Bob hits the pause button, catches his breath and refuels, recognising that, in order to get back onto the Century 21 Business Treadmill and stay upright, he'll have to somehow up his game.

He knows he's in the right place to do just that – there's a track around the gym to build his stamina away from the treadmill, lots of free advice and a whole selection of tools to help him hit his target.

He's also aware that when it comes to working through the Recession Setting on the Century 21 Business Treadmill, a couple of steps back aren't wasted if you're using them as a run-up to the next big marker.

That's why he's been a member of the Sales Gym so long. He's watched too many newbies step up and fall over – **his advice is always there, if they need it; some ask, most don't.**

He smiles as he picks up his bag to leave and reads the motto above the front door:

"Change yourself and fortune will change with you."

A Sales Fairy Tale to Send You on Your Way

Once upon a time there was a Sales King who had two beautiful children who gave him great joy: Prospect and Customa. Great fortunes were spent on them and many songs were sung.

One night they were put to bed, while the Sales King filled his time with inconsequential nonsense and, although he'd promised to tuck them in tight, he knew where they were and that they would always be waiting for him whenever he found the time to pass by and give them some attention.

The Time Demon watched on, laughing at the King's stupidity, and then – just to be mean – decided to suck all recognition of the passing of hours from the King's chambers.

Prospect and Customa became sad, believing that the King had forgotten all about them, and so started to wish that someone would care for them properly and listen to the things they were so desperate to say. As they considered what might be, their minds wandered.

When the spell was eventually broken, the Sales King jumped from his throne in horror, as he realised how foolish he had been. He shouted for the cleverest man in the land to come and give him guidance. *"What shall I do?"* he wailed. *"How do I make this right?"*

"Pull yourself together, you fool!" advised the old man wisely. *"Get up and go to see them both before it's too late; you really have no idea how precious Prospect and Customa are to everyone in the kingdom – not least of all to your enemies, who would happily steal them away and treat them extremely badly."*

"Well, that would never do," declared the King. *"We need a plan."*

"Here's a plan," instructed the wise old sage. *"Make sure that you look after Prospect and Customa like the royalty they are; protect them like your most valuable possessions and then keep every promise you ever make to them. For if they ever decide to leave you, they will probably never return. Feel free to follow the advice of wolves who think nothing of devouring defenceless grandmothers if you wish, and by all means, carry on searching for the magic beans that might make you rich or a love potion that promises to control the hearts and minds of others – but do so in the knowledge that the wolves and the peddlers of potions do not care for you or your future, only themselves."*

With that, the wise man was gone, leaving the King alone to consider his future.

After following the old man's advice for only a few short weeks, he accidentally stumbled across the words that spelled out the secret of success. He found them interwoven with the hopes and dreams of his wonderful Prospect and Customa. And once he'd recognised that, the Gods decided to bless him with countless years of happiness and contentment, until his Kingdom became an Empire.

FURTHER RECOMMENDED READING

(in no particular order)

Secrets of Closing the Sale by Zig Ziglar

The Sales Bible by Jeffrey Gitomer

Fanatical Prospecting by Jeb Blount

80/20 Sales and Marketing by Perry Marshall

Think and Grow Rich by Napoleon Hill

Purple Cow by Seth Godin

The Greatest Salesman in the World by Og Mandino

25 Habits of Highly Successful Salespeople by Stephan Schiffman

The Challenger Sale by Matthew Dixon and Brent Adamson

Spin Selling by Neil Rackham

Snap Selling by Jill Konrath

People Buy You by Jeb Blount

Brilliant Selling by Tom Bird and Jeremy Cassell

Cold Calling Techniques by Stephan Schiffman

Major Account Sales Strategy by Neil Rackham

To Sell is Human by Daniel H Pink

Advanced Selling Strategies by Brian Tracy

Selling to Win by Richard Denny

How to Master the Art of Selling by Tom Hopkins

The Negotiation Book by Steve Gates

Selling to Big Companies by Jill Konrath

How to Sell by Jo Owen

The New Strategic Selling by Robert B Miller, Stephen E Heiman and Tad Tuleja

Sell or Be Sold by Grant Cordone

The Extremely Successful Salesman's Club by Chris Murray

About the Author

Chris Murray is founder and Managing Director of the **Varda Kreuz Training Group** and has become prominent as an inspirational speaker, author and business coach; delivering training workshops and keynote speeches that challenge teams to re-examine what it means to be *'in sales'* and requiring them to stand back and view the whole experience from a refreshingly different angle.

His books include **The Extremely Successful Salesman's Club** – which was an Amazon Number 1 Best Seller heralded as the Da Vinci Code for salespeople – and **The Managers Guide to Achieving FAME**.

He has also written and contributed to articles for a number of institutions, magazines and websites including; the Institute of Sales and Marketing Management, Training Magazine Europe, The Sales Pro, CNBC.com, Entrepreneur, The Huffington Post and USA Today.

The Varda Kreuz Training Group

The Varda Kreuz ethos has always been based on delivering training that really works. Not in theory and not just sometimes, training that really works.

Every business has its own unique challenges, and although your everyday issues might not necessarily be original, they will almost certainly be bespoke - so it's our firm belief that your training and professional development should be too.

We specialise in sales, management and customer service training – and take great pride in the fact that we are not just another, faceless corporate training company delivering generic, uninspiring, workaday courses.

We are Varda Kreuz.

www.vardakreuztraining.com
info@vardakreuztraining.com